THE WILDERNESS COOKBOOK

A GUIDE TO GOOD FOOD ON THE TRAIL

*The Ultimate Meal Planner
with Menu Guides
and Camping Tips*

THE WILDERNESS COOKBOOK

A Guide to Good Food on the Trail

by
Bonnie McTaggart
&
Jill Bryant

Illustrated by
Chum McLeod

SECOND STORY *Press*

CANADIAN CATALOGUING IN PUBLICATION
McTaggart, Bonnie, 1942-
The wilderness cookbook: a guide to
good food on the trail

ISBN 1-896764-18-5

1. Outdoor cookery. 2. Camping — Equipment and supplies.
I. Bryant, Jill. II. McLeod, Chum. III. Title.

TX823.M297 1999   641.5'78   C99-930370-8

Edited by Dianne Broad and Samantha Simpson
Illustrated by Chum McLeod

Printed and bound in Canada
This book is printed on acid-free paper.

*Second Story Press gratefully acknowledges the
financial support of the Government of Canada through the
Book Publishing Industry Development Program.*

*We gratefully acknowledge the support of Webcom Limited's
Unpublished Authors Sweepstakes Program.*

Published by
SECOND STORY PRESS
720 Bathurst Street, Suite 301
Toronto, Ontario
M5S 2R4

To all of the canoe trippers, backpackers,
hunters, and cyclists with heavy loads:
Hope this helps you out!

To all of the friends who have accompanied us on canoe trips
and contributed advice on improving the recipes and simplifying campsite
chores. We look forward to many more trips with you.
P.S.: You have to keep washing the dishes!

To Shirley Keele, who has done her last canoe trip.
She will always be our role model for the "best attitude."

And to Gramma Mary/Mom, who is an inspiration to us all
for her remarkable achievements.

— B. M. & J. B.

ACKNOWLEDGMENTS

Special thanks to the Davisons for allowing us the use of
their idyllic setting for our co-operative writing sessions;
Joyce George, our friendly neighbour with the expert
food advice; John Gilbert, who taught us every single one
of his camping tips; and, of course, Pete McTaggart and
Daryn Lehoux, who exemplify the saying, "The way
to a man's heart is through his stomach!"

CONTENTS

INTRODUCTION

WHEN WE FIRST began going on canoe trips we found that we had a very limited number of meals we could cook in the wilderness. Most of our friends prepared hasty meals from canned foods such as spaghetti and beans. While these dinners did provide some food value, they lacked creativity and were back-breakingly heavy. It's true that even the most uninteresting food can taste remarkably good when you've been outside all day, but if you approach outdoor cooking with a creative mind, you can look forward to mealtime on the trail as a high point of the day.

By adapting wholesome cooking techniques, Bonnie McTaggart has created an extensive collection of practical, well-rounded meals. You'll be surprised at how she combines everyday kitchen methods with deep-woods ambiance and campfire flavour. The results are delicious!

On one memorable women's canoe trip, which included three generations of our family, we decided that we would create a cookbook devoted to backpackers and canoe trippers to share Bonnie's economical and easy-to-carry trail recipes with other nature enthusiasts. Jill Bryant, with her writing and editing experience, was appointed as the co-writer to organize the recipes into a logical format and round it out into a full-fledged book. Thus, our mother-and-daughter team was born!

The entourage for our multi-generational canoe trip was as follows:

- MARY McLEOD (mother and grandmother), 75 years old at the time of this trip, who instilled in us her love of wholesome home cooking. Mary still cooks on a woodstove in her stone farmhouse, and, not surprisingly, was the best in the group at collecting dry wood for our campfire.

- BONNIE McTAGGART (mother, daughter, and sister), who adapted good nutrition and cooking techniques to wilderness outings. Using limited camping equipment, she produced a delicious meal every time. Bonnie's preference for vegetarian meals and low-fat recipes results in healthful, high-energy foods that help you perform well and feel great during your wilderness trips.

- CHUM McLEOD (sister, daughter, and aunt), who won the "best-dressed" award with her Aztec-inspired fleece jacket and her never-ending selection of colourful hand-knit socks. You'll enjoy Chum's zany, evocative illustrations throughout this book.

- JILL BRYANT (daughter, niece, and granddaughter), who apprenticed under Bonnie, stirring the pot and dropping dumplings into the bubbling stew. Jill was usually the first one to lick her plate clean in appreciation of Bonnie's creations.

- NANCY KNUDSTRUP (friend), who volunteered to be the official taster for the book. Nancy was responsible for many of the more thought-provoking discussions at our campfire tête-à-têtes.

- TOBY the dog, who kept us alert by disturbing the calm of our tranquil paddling with his many wet leaps in and out of the water. He tested our packing techniques by taking every opportunity to plop his usually wet 35-kilogram mass right on top of our food pack in the canoe! When dinnertime arrived, Toby was always nearby with his wagging tail and hopeful countenance. He didn't get any leftovers, however — we always ate everything!

During one of our particularly scrumptious curry dinners, we decided, as a group, to create a cookbook for both novice and experienced wilderness campers who, like us, love the outdoors and enjoy easy-to-make, hearty meals. We have provided a full range of simple and tasty meals for people who like — or would like — to get away from the conveniences available at many campgrounds and still enjoy a great meal at the end of each day. The dinners are substantial enough to accommodate increased "outdoor" appetites, but in their dehydrated state they are light-weight and easy to carry. Reasonably priced ingredients are also a consideration. You'll notice a balance of old favourites and comfort foods with more diverse international recipes. And if you're camping with children, you'll appreciate the recipes that were created especially with children in mind! The book is much more than just recipes; we've also included preparation advice, packing suggestions, safety tips, and lots of funny stories about our personal experiences in the wilderness.

With a little preparation and pre-trip organization, you'll be well equipped to serve a wide variety of delicious meals that are sure to energize your group for another active day. Since very few dehydrated vegetables are available commercially, you will achieve the best results if you dry your own vegetables at home. And if you're pressed for time, we've also included *Quick Dinners* and *A Very Easy Weekend Trip* plan. These quick recipes, adapted for busy people, use some of the instant convenience foods that are available at grocery stores, but we have enhanced their nutritional value wherever possible. The recipes listed under *Basic Dinners* will really dazzle your companions.

Welcome to a new approach to travelling light and eating fabulous, healthful meals in the woods! Enjoy!

Bonnie McTaggart and Jill Bryant

Starting Off

All of our dinner recipes are designed to make hearty, protein-complete meals that provide maximum energy after a day of physical exertion. The meals contain combinations of starch, grains, milk products, nuts, beans — and lots of vegetables! We have provided options for including various types of meat, but the focus of the book is vegetarian. The foods we have chosen are based on the following criteria:

1) durability
2) compactness
3) lightweight
4) excellent nutritional value
5) reasonable cooking and preparation time
6) great taste
7) low cost

The cost for food per person is about $10 per day using the dehydration recipes described in this book. This per-day rate includes three meals, snacks, and drinks.

Suggested Cooking Equipment and Utensils

All of the recipes can be made on a campfire or gas campstove using a basic set of stackable camping cookware. A cook-pot set for four people is the most functional size for a group of two to six people. We found that the smaller size was too small and awkward for even two people. Most of the recipes in this book require a

large pot and are designed to feed four hungry people. Camping-supply stores offer four-person-size aluminum cook sets for about $30, while a stainless-steel/copper-bottom set with three pots will cost $50 to $80.

Most basic cook sets include one large pot (about 6 quarts or 6 L) with a lid, two small pots, and four to six plates and cups. The pot lid can also double as a frying pan to reduce extra weight, but you may find that including a heavier frying pan in your supply pack will make camp cooking easier. You can purchase metal, enamel, or heavy plastic mugs, plates, and cheap cutlery in a discount store or a camping-supply store if they aren't included in the cook set. Try to get stackable mugs — other types will take up a lot of room in your pack.

We also recommend carrying your own grill because it is often missing at campsites. By using a grill instead of uneven platforms of rock, you will reduce the risk of losing your dinner to the cinders. A small size — about 12" by 22" (30 cm by 55 cm) — is sufficient. Our current grill was salvaged from an old gas barbeque.

These cooking supplies — cook set and grill — are the basic equipment for preparing all of the meals in this book. Altogether, these supplies can weigh three to five pounds (1.36 to 2.27 kg) — not an unreasonable weight for a portable kitchen! You can decide what other useful utensils you want to take. For example, a pot grip or an old oven mitt is handy for removing hot pots from the

On an unbelievable first canoe trip together, Daryn and I forgot our entire cook set! In desperation, we borrowed an old beat-up dog dish from a cottager, which we used for boiling our pasta. We used a mini-can opener — which we had remembered — to remove the top from an empty pop can and used this to make single cups of tea.   – *Jill*

fire. When packing utensils, remember that the less you bring the lighter your load, but also consider your menu plan when packing utensils. There's nothing worse than forgetting a flipper when you plan to make pancakes, or overlooking a can opener when you plan to enhance your meal with canned tuna.

Some basic equipment would include:

- four-person cook set (mark pots with a line at the 4-cup/1-L, 6-cup/1.5-L, 8-cup/2-L water levels to simplify measuring at the campsite)
- campstove (essential during rainy weather or imposed fire restrictions)
- fuel for stove (always take some extra)
- plates
- cups (mark at the 1-cup/250-mL level to measure water for cooking and baking)
- cutlery
- frying pan (optional if your pot lid converts to a frying pan)
- sharp knife/penknife (for slicing cheese and fresh vegetables)
- grill
- large serving spoon (optional)
- can opener (only if you are packing cans)
- metal pancake flipper (only if required for recipes)
- pot grip holder (sometimes comes with cook set; can use oven mitt instead)

- matches (keep two supplies in separate locations)
- oven mitt (optional — you can use an old towel)
- tea towel (endless uses — especially for draining pasta)
- newspaper for starting fire (just a few sheets for starting fires under wet conditions. Store in a ziplock bag inside your food pack inside the plastic liner. This paper will only be useful if it is kept dry. Once a fire is started it is possible to add wet wood and keep it burning.)
- diffuser (helps to prevent burning and sticking on the bottom of the pot or frying pan, and is especially helpful for baking; can be purchased in camping-supply stores)

TIPS FOR SPONTANEOUS TRIPS

If you know you'll be very busy during the summer, try to make extra dried meals in advance. Then, if you decide to embark on a spontaneous trip, you'll have a head start on your preparation. When properly packaged and sealed, meals will keep in the refrigerator for up to six months.

If you are canoe tripping and will be staying at one base camp for the whole trip, weight will probably not be a prime consideration for your wilderness outing. In such cases you can plan meals that use some canned goods since you can pack out compressed cans with your garbage. However, for trips such as hiking, which require you to carry your food, we don't advise taking canned goods. Instead, eliminate carrying the weight and bulk of heavy cans and fresh produce by dehydrating your fruit and vegetables and contents of your canned goods in advance.

Before You Leave Home

Some of the food preparation must be done at home before you leave. Each dinner is assembled, packaged, and labelled for easy identification when you're on the trail. The cooking instructions for each dinner are copied at home and inserted in each dinner package so you know what to do with your packaged ingredients when you get to your campsite. (Or you can take this book with you — we've designed it to be lightweight and portable. Carry it in a ziplock bag to keep it dry.) You'll then be able to prepare the breakfasts and lunches quickly on the trail with a small campstove. However, if you choose to stay at one campsite for a day of relaxation, and decide to make a morning campfire, we have also included lazy-day campfire breakfasts. Freshly baked blueberry muffins and a cup of coffee or tea — that's what camp cooks strive to perfect!

This book provides you with a checklist for foods that we have adapted for wilderness meals, with recipes for breakfast, lunch, dinner, dessert, and snacks. We have also provided a checklist for all of the cooking-related equipment you'll need (see page *157*). We've kept in mind that you may carry the food pack and camping gear for at least part of your trip. Through food dehydration and careful menu planning, the weight of food is kept to a minimum.

The book also outlines dinner menus for about 20 completely different basic meals and also provides many variations and serving options so you can have a wide variety of meals to suit the duration of your wilderness trip and your personal food preferences. You can learn how to create your own dinner recipes as well with our simple chart and instructions (see page *142–144*). Adapt a favourite "at home" meal for your wilderness needs or personalize our recipes.

You may want to purchase a large pack for storing all of the food together and use a separate backpack for your clothing and other articles. Having all of the food for your group in one designated pack will make it easier to quickly locate the ingredients for your meals. You can hang the food pack in a safe location after finishing your dinner and still have all your warm sweaters, mosquito repellent, and toothbrushes ready for use throughout the evening.

A pack with some outside pockets eases accessibility to frequently needed items, such as drink crystals and trail mix. With dehydrated food, it is quite possible to carry all of the food for four people for a six-day wilderness canoe trip in one standard-sized (50- to 60-L) pack. We use an old backpack with lots of outside pockets. Line the pack with a large, leakproof plastic bag to keep everything dry. (Remember Toby the dog who loves to get comfortable on top of the food pack in the canoe — especially when he is soaking wet!) If you are hiking, on the other hand, you will want to distribute the food among all of the hikers in your group.

Making Your Own Dried Food

PREPARING YOUR OWN dried food at home provides you with nutritious, lightweight, and compact meals with no additives. You will also have more control over the salt and sugar content, and will save money compared to purchasing freeze-dried or commercially prepared dehydrated foods. For example, a two-serving package of commercially dehydrated peas costs more than three dollars. Freeze-dried foods are even more expensive and are also more bulky; however, freeze-dried foods are the quickest to rehydrate at your campsite. Regardless of whether you dry your own foods or purchase commercially prepared or freeze-dried ones, you will rehydrate them at the campsite (by soaking them in water). When they are rehydrated, you'll be impressed by their plumpness, juiciness, and attractive appearance. The drying process reduces 80 to 90 per cent of the water in vegetables. This not only greatly reduces the weight and bulk of the food, but also preserves the product, which is necessary for wilderness conditions. If you were to assemble cans, fresh produce, and the rest of the ingredients to make chili, for example, the weight is about 7 pounds (3 kg). When dehydrated, the result is significantly more compact and the weight is less than 1½ pounds (0.75 kg).

Vegetables are naturally high in vitamins, fibre, and minerals, and low in fat. Surprisingly, none of the nutrients are lost when vegetables are properly dried. If the temperature is too high and the vegetables are burnt, however, the nutritional value of the food will decrease just as it would with any other type of preparation.

You can use two different home methods for drying vegetables: oven drying or food-dehydrator drying. If you are a novice, oven drying will suffice for your needs. Once you have established your commitment to, and need for, dried food, you might decide to invest in a food dehydrator.

FRESH PRODUCE OPTIONS

Fresh produce enhances any meal, but it is often too heavy, perishable, and bulky to carry in large quantities. Most of our dinner recipes include various dehydrated vegetables. When they are rehydrated (by soaking in water at the campsite), you'll be amazed at their plump juiciness and impressive visual appeal. Nevertheless, you may want to purchase a few fresh fruits and vegetables that can be shared at lunches. Carrots, cucumbers, firm pears, apples, and oranges are the least perishable (and least squishable) varieties of produce to include. Decide how much fresh produce each person will eat each day. Because of weight, you will probably want to minimize the quantity. For example, you might allot one carrot or apple to each person per day.

Carefully pack fresh foods near the top of your pack. Make sure they aren't on top of your bread or under your frying pan. For the first night out, you may want to try your luck with more perishable and bulky foods such as bananas, peaches, or melon, especially if you are simply pitching camp beside your car or paddling a very short distance before nightfall.

Preparing Vegetables

Always choose fresh, high-quality vegetables. Slice or cut the vegetables into uniform sizes (for each type) so that drying will occur at the same time for each variety of vegetable. An ideal thickness is ⅛" (3 mm). The following list comprises all of the vegetables that are called for in the recipes found in this cookbook; however, it is possible to dehydrate many other types of vegetables. For example, you can even dehydrate green leafy vegetables such as spinach, chard, and kale. As you gain experience and also experiment with drying foods, you'll want to try using vegetables that we haven't included in our recipes.

You will notice that the following list doesn't include dehydrated potatoes. We don't recommend dehydrating potatoes for a variety of reasons. First, commercially prepared potato flakes and potato slices are inexpensive and readily available. Second, our attempts at dehydrating potatoes have resulted in an unappealing, discoloured product. Finally, potatoes require an unusually lengthy period for dehydrating.

Black beans, canned – rinse, drain, and pat dry
Carrots – slice thinly or grate
Cauliflower – steam for one minute and slice thinly
Celery – slice thinly
Chickpeas, canned – rinse, drain, and pat dry
Corn, frozen – thaw, pat dry
Green beans, frozen – thaw, pat dry
Kidney beans, canned – rinse, drain, and pat dry
Mushrooms – slice thinly

Navy beans, canned – rinse, drain, and pat dry
Onion – sliver
Peas, frozen – thaw, pat dry
Peppers – cut into julienne strips
Snow peas – steam for one minute
Zucchini – slice thinly

If you are using fresh peas, corn, or beans, blanch them for one minute in boiling water, chill in cold water, pat dry, and proceed with drying instructions. If you are using frozen products, the blanching process has already been done.

DEHYDRATOR METHOD

Most dehydrating machines have different settings for drying fruit, vegetables, and meat, and have several layers of drying racks. Follow the instructions for your particular model. When making leathers, be sure to cover the drying rack with plastic wrap to prevent the purée from seeping through.

OVEN-DRYING METHOD

It is easier and faster to dry food when the weather is not too humid. We recommend drying your food several days or a week before leaving on your trip as it takes about one day to dry the food for each dinner. This may seem like a lot of time for one meal, but the only real work involves a few minutes of chopping. Granted, the drying process does require time (about 8 to 10 hours), but it certainly isn't labour intensive. Furthermore, preparing meals in advance will leave you with enough time to organize your camping gear, cooking utensils, and clothing.

- Preheat the oven at the lowest temperature setting. In most ovens the top element only comes on during preheating or broiling, so you will be able to use both racks for drying (i.e., the heat will come from the bottom element). If your oven's top element comes on again, however, you might have to use an empty baking tray or a sheet of aluminum foil to shield the food from the top element.
- Place the prepared fruit or vegetables on ungreased baking sheets.
- Place the baking sheets in the oven. Make sure the thin slices are only one layer thick, are well spaced, and do not touch each other.
- Use a wooden spoon to prop the door open 1" to 2" (3 to 5 cm) to keep the temperature down and allow air circulation.
- Every hour or so, stir the vegetables or fruit to prevent sticking.
- Because the temperature can vary within the oven, from time to time rotate the trays from back to front. (During this process do not leave trays outside the oven for any length of time because moulds can form easily on partly dried foods that are left at room temperature. For this reason, it is important to set aside the time required to complete the drying process.)
- Check the vegetables more often towards the end of the process to avoid scorching or burning.
- Some vegetables dehydrate more quickly than others. When the vegetables are dry, remove the sheets from the oven and transfer the vegetables to paper towels until they are completely cool. Check carefully for doneness.
- Cool completely before packing.
- Pack each type of dried vegetable separately. Use plastic baggies (not ziplock bags, which are bulkier) and remove as much air as possible from the bags. Store in the refrigerator.

To speed up the drying process, you can stretch aluminum screening over the oven rack. Place the vegetables directly on the screening and proceed with oven drying. This method allows more air circulation in the oven. Screening is available at hardware stores. Just make sure you don't use the plastic kind!

Dryness Test

Once the vegetables have been in the oven for several hours, it is important to test for dryness. Most vegetables (such as green beans, celery, onions, peas, corn, chickpeas, and snow peas) should be brittle when they are dried properly. Other vegetables (such as carrots, mushrooms, peppers, tomatoes, zucchini, and cauliflower) are leathery in texture. Test one piece by allowing it to cool to room temperature before establishing the degree of dryness. (Warm food will be more pliable than cool food.) If the test piece is not dry enough when it is cool, continue drying the remaining vegetables and then repeat the test. Most vegetables will take 8 to 10 hours to dry; some, such as onions, take even longer.

Recognizing the correct degree of dryness is a skill you will learn with a bit of practice. If you are in doubt, dry a little longer as it is safer to overdry than underdry.

As you gain experience with drying vegetables and understand how your oven works, you can experiment with drying overnight. Even then, however, it's a good idea for someone to be home the next day because the drying process might take even longer. Our advice: experiment, experiment, experiment — and don't become discouraged if you initially have problems. Persevere: the results are well worth it. Remember — drying is an age-old process practised by our ancestors with only very limited equipment.

Making Leathers

Tomato Leather

You've probably heard of fruit leather, but what in the world is "tomato" leather? This ingenious roll-up food rehydrates to become a flavourful tomato sauce. Unlike fruit leather, it is not meant to be a snack food; instead, tomato leather is rehydrated and used for the liquid base for some dinners.

Making your own tomato leather eliminates the need for cans and greatly reduces weight. The leather softens and rehydrates easily at the campsite. You can prepare tomato leather from canned tomato sauce, tomato paste, or a combination of the two — depending on the requirements of your recipe.

•Preheat the oven at the lowest temperature possible.

- Cover a baking sheet (or aluminum screening) with plastic wrap. (Don't worry — the oven temperature is low enough that the plastic wrap won't melt all over the inside of the oven.)
- Pour the tomato sauce or paste (or a mixture of the two) onto the plastic wrap. If you will be using tomato leather in more than one of the recipes used for your excursion, double or triple the amount accordingly. If you are doubling the amount, use two sheets and make two smaller leathers. This will dry more quickly than using one large tray.
- Smooth out the tomato sauce or paste. Using the back of a spoon or a spatula, spread the mixture evenly to facilitate uniform drying. It should be less than ¼" (0.5 cm) thick.
- Dry for 8 to 10 hours. Check the leather often towards the end of the process to avoid burning it. Burnt tomato leather will give your meal a bitter flavour. (We don't recommend leaving the leather in the oven overnight to dry, since burnt tomato leather will ruin your entire meal.)
- When the leather is well dried on the top and around the edges, remove it from the oven and peel the leather back from the plastic wrap. Turn the leather over on the baking sheet and place it back in the oven. Discard the plastic wrap.
- Finish drying the tomato leather until it feels supple and resembles leather — likely another two or three hours. It may seem too soft at this stage, but let it cool slightly and check whether it then resembles leather.
- Roll the tomato leather into a compact log and store it in a sealed plastic bag in the refrigerator.

FRUIT LEATHER

Chewy, flavourful, nutritious, and sweet, fruit leathers are both easy to make and economical. Children especially love them. Fruit leathers are made from fruit that is cooked for a few minutes with enough water to prevent scorching. Sugar is not usually needed as the natural sugars of the fruit are concentrated during this process. If the fruit tastes sweet enough in its puréed state, it will be sweet enough for the leather.
- Preheat the oven at the lowest temperature possible.
- Wash and dry the fruit. Remove any bruised or blemished parts of the fruit. If you are using fruits such as apples, peaches, or bananas, peel the fruit. Cut the fruit into small chunks. Add a

little water. (Adding 1 tbsp/15 mL lemon juice will also prevent the fruit from darkening.)

- Place the fruit in a saucepan and cook over low/medium heat for 5 to 10 minutes. Purée or mash the fruit with a fork. It should be about the consistency of thick applesauce. If it is too runny, remove the lid and simmer the fruit for a few minutes longer. Don't overcook or you will lose the flavour.
- Taste for sweetness. Add sugar if necessary.
- Spread the puréed fruit onto plastic wrap that is stretched over a baking sheet. Smooth it out as evenly as possible to facilitate uniform drying. It should be less than ¼" (0.5 cm) thick.
  Note: 1½ cups (375 mL) of fruit pulp will make a 9" x 9" (23 cm x 23 cm) square.
- Dry for 8 to 10 hours in a dehydrator or oven (see *Oven-Drying Method*, page 22).
- When the fruit leather is dry around the edges, remove it from the oven and peel it from the plastic wrap. Turn the leather over on the baking sheet and place it back in the oven. Discard the plastic wrap. Dry the fruit for about 2 more hours or until it is the consistency of leather. Thinner areas around the edge may become quite brittle.
- Cool, roll up, and store in the refrigerator in a sealed plastic bag.

VARIOUS FRUIT OPTIONS:

1) If you use only apples, you may need to add a small amount of sugar — 1 to 2 tsp (5 mL to 10 mL) per cup (250 mL) of purée.

2) Apples make an excellent base into which other fruits may be added. Combine with plums, peaches, apricots, and so on. Just put both prepared fruits together, and proceed as above.

3) Berries, such as raspberries, strawberries, and currants, add wonderful flavour to the apple base. Cook the berries separately with a very small amount of water. Remove the seeds by pressing the cooked berry pulp through a sieve and then adding the seedless pulp to the prepared apple mixture. Stir to combine and add sugar to taste.

4) Banana leather is delicious and easy to make. Begin by mashing some ripe bananas and then purée the mash. Lemon juice may be added for extra flavour and to help preserve the colour. Sesame seeds can be sprinkled over the purée after it is spread out on some plastic wrap.

Banana slices or quarters can be dried to make banana chips or sticks. Just slice or quarter the banana and arrange pieces on the drying tray so they don't touch each other. Dry until they are leathery.

TEXTURED VEGETABLE PROTEIN

Textured vegetable protein (TVP) is a commercially dried vegetarian product that comes in several different forms including granular or cubed. It is easily rehydrated and adds nutritional value and chewiness to meals. TVP can be added to many one-pot meals.

MEAT PRODUCTS

You can add meat to most of the dinner recipes by including homemade or commercially prepared meat products. The following types of meat are preserved and provide excellent options for canoeing and hiking trips:

- beef jerky
- dried chicken, beef, or turkey
- pepperoni sausage
- summer sausage (cloth-bag variety)

Unlike homemade dried ground beef, or jerky, these products do not have to soak in water to rehydrate. (Follow the instructions on any commercially dried product.) However, remember that these commercially preserved meats are concentrated and are often very high in additives, fat, and salt. Try to use in moderation: one small pepperoni sausage can enhance a dinner, adding good flavour and heartiness.

DRYING GROUND BEEF

For all ground-beef variations indicated in our recipes, use the following method of drying and cooking:

- Preheat the oven at the lowest temperature possible.
- In an ungreased frying pan, cook lean ground beef over medium-high heat. It is very important to start out with lean beef as the fat can turn rancid very quickly out on the trail if the weather is extremely hot and humid.

- When the ground beef is browned and all of the fat has drained off, remove it from the heat. Pour off any excess fat and then drain the ground meat on paper towels to remove any leftover fat. Pat the meat dry.
- Transfer the ground beef onto fresh paper towels, cover with paper towels and place it in the microwave oven for 2 to 3 minutes on the regular setting. This process will remove even more fat. If you do not have a microwave oven, take extra care with the previous step, removing all traces of visible fat and draining it well.
- Cover a baking sheet with paper towels. Spread the ground beef evenly over the paper towels and place it in the oven (or food dehydrator) for several hours. When completely dry, the beef should be very hard and brittle and won't resemble meat.
- Cool the dried ground beef thoroughly and wrap it in a heavy plastic bag. Store it in the refrigerator.

At Campsite:
- The ground beef will rehydrate when water is added at the campsite. We recommend cooking the beef with the meal for at least 30 minutes. The texture of the meat may be slightly different from what you eat at home, but the flavour will be the same.

> If your meat has "gone off" because there was too much fat remaining after the drying process, you will definitely know. Rancid meat has a very unpleasant smell. Don't worry about accidentally eating bad meat. You'll know before you even think of sampling it! Phew! As we discussed earlier, you can avoid this by carefully following the steps outlined above.

MAKING BEEF JERKY

- Preheat the oven at the lowest temperature possible.
- Choose a very lean cut of meat, such as flank steak.
- Slice the meat into very thin strips, which is easier to do if you freeze the meat slightly.
- Add soy sauce or herbs, or salt and pepper, if desired.
- Place the prepared meat on ungreased baking sheets. Make sure the slices are only one layer thick, are well spaced, and do not touch each other.
- Place in the oven for several hours — likely 12 to 16 hours.

(You can also use a food dehydrator.)
- Cool the jerky thoroughly and package it in a plastic bag.
- Store in the refrigerator. Always wrap the jerky separately from other foods.

<small></small>

AT CAMPSITE:
- The beef jerky will rehydrate when water is added at the campsite. As with rehydrated ground beef, the texture of the rehydrated jerky may be slightly different, but the flavour is unchanged. You can also use beef jerky as a snack food.

Note: Boneless, skinless chicken or turkey can be substituted for beef in the above recipe.

When you rehydrate food at the campsite, you can use untreated water because the cooking process requires 30 minutes of boiling time. This cooking time is more than sufficient to kill any harmful bacteria. However, in cases where you don't cook the rehydrated food (such as coleslaw), then you must use treated water. For a more detailed discussion about water, see page 47.

IMPLEMENTATION

Now that you understand the principles of drying foods, we'll look at how you prepare your meals in advance and organize your supplies.

For each wilderness outing, choose the dinners from the selection offered, including your chosen options. Remember to consider your group's needs — food allergies, food preferences, number of people, and appetite levels. We have found it practical to have a separate piece of paper for each dinner, with all of the ingredients carefully listed. This proves useful when packing, to ensure that you remember all of the ingredients. For example, for a three-day trip you might choose the following dinners:

Stew with Dumplings
Spaghetti with Vegetables and Tomato Sauce
Moroccan Couscous

List all of the ingredients for each dinner. Use a separate piece of paper for each meal.

Then review the lists and determine how many batches of dried vegetables you will need. In this way, you can group all of the same vegetables together to streamline the drying process. For example, for the meals listed above, you will need:

- carrots for two dinners
- zucchini for two dinners
- tomato leather for two dinners

Then, after dehydrating the vegetables, divide the dried product into the portions required.

Assemble each dinner according to your list and check the ingredients off each list as you pack. Package each dried vegetable individually in a baggie. Assemble herbs, spices, and seasonings in a baggie. Package everything together in a heavy plastic bag, including the campsite instructions, and label the package with the name of the dinner and the day you wish to serve it, if applicable.

Cooking and Camping Tips

Campstove vs. Campfire

Before you leave, decide whether you will be cooking by campstove or campfire, or both. If you are unsure about whether campfires are allowed in the area you will be visiting, you can find out about any fire restrictions by contacting the local tourism board. If there are severe fire restrictions, you absolutely cannot have a fire and the area will likely be monitored by helicopter to ensure that no one breaks the rules. Fire restrictions are enforced during periods of drought, when forest fires are likely to occur, and in particularly sensitive areas of old-growth forest. If you won't be able to use a campfire, you might want to choose meals that require less cooking time. If you will be using a campstove exclusively, however, you must determine how much camp fuel you will need — and always bring a little extra. You might decide to bring two small campstoves if you have a group of four or more people.

The minimum required cooking times are given in our dinner recipes. Meals can be prepared on a campstove, but you may find that you achieve better results over a fire. Longer cooking will enhance the flavour if this does not compromise your time or fuel restrictions.

Be aware of the human effect on the area you are visiting and try to minimize it. Our rule of thumb is to use a fire only where a fire pit is already established; this prevents unnecessary scarring. In any ecologically sensitive area, such as in old-growth forests or above the treeline, you should avoid campfires altogether.

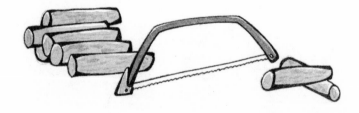

Setting Up a Cook Station

When you arrive at your campsite, transform your canoe into a practical piece of furniture by turning it over and using it as a table or work surface. Find a level area near your fire and stabilize the overturned canoe with stones. Dishes, utensils, and any non-food items can be stored and kept dry underneath it at night.

You can purchase wood directly from the park authorities or collect pieces of dead, fallen wood from the forest floor. If you choose the latter, do so sparingly, for minimal disruption of the surrounding ecosystem. Never cut down trees for firewood; live trees won't burn and such acts damage the environment. A small, stiff-bladed saw works better than an axe for cutting lengths of wood for the fire. Saws are also lighter than axes and generally safer.

Stack your wood upwind from the fire pit and cover it with a plastic sheet. Always assume that it will rain overnight. Even if it doesn't rain, there is often a heavy dew that will make your wood wet. Build up the fire-pit stones to fit your grill. By stacking the stones on three sides you will protect the fire from the wind. The grill must sit as level as possible to provide a stable cooking surface. A height of 8" to 10" (about 20 cm to 25 cm) from the grill to the bottom of the fire pit is ideal. Once you have established how the grill fits, you can remove it when you begin to build the fire. Let the fire burn into a low bed of coals and then add the grill when

you are ready to start cooking. Through practice, you will learn to regulate the temperature of the fire with almost the same confidence as switching on your electric stove at home — and it's a lot more fun! Generally, a low fire with a hot bed of coals will provide the best heat for simmering your food. To boil water, build up the fire so the flames lick the bottom of the pot. Put a lid on the pot to accelerate the boiling process. If the fire is too hot, just move the pot to the edge of the grill. Start your fire early, while the vegetables are rehydrating, so that the fire is ready to cook when you are.

Leaving a Cook Station

One of the last and crucially important campsite duties is to pour several buckets of water over the campfire before you leave to ensure that you don't inadvertently start a forest fire. The large pot is ideal for this purpose.

Recycle your empty, leakproof containers. Rinse them and put them in a designated spot in your food pack. We usually store them in an outside pocket.

Emergency Food Supplies

Depending on your degree of isolation in the wilderness, we recommend packing some emergency rations such as extra powdered soups, drink crystals, hot chocolate, and instant hot cereal. While it is unlikely that you will get lost in the bush, delays due to inclement weather are possible, and it will be reassuring to know that you have some extra supplies. Because you will be carrying all of your food, most people tend to underpack rather than overpack. With experience, however, you will learn to pack the right amount of food, balancing the voracious wilderness appetites of long hard days with the more snack-oriented cravings of lazy days on a beach. On an ideal trip, your emergency rations will be the only food that you bring home.

It's quite amusing to experience the diminishing size and weight of the food pack as the days pass. On the first night, it might take three people to hang the food pack in a tree: one person to haul on the rope and two people to push the heavy bag up into the air. As your trip progresses, however, the food pack becomes lighter.

By the last day, after your last lunch, you'll laugh at the small crumpled bag of odds and ends that is now the food pack.

OVERNIGHT SAFETY

The most common nocturnal visitor to campsites in Ontario is the raccoon. Although they are usually harmless, they have been known to scavenge through poorly hung packs for any food they can get their paws on. For this reason, be especially vigilant when preparing and storing your food. For example, if you open a can of tuna, salmon, or sardines, be careful where you pour the oil or water. If this liquid falls on the ground near your campsite, animals may be attracted to the area. Instead, bury any excess oil.

Don't ignore the existence of those big brown or black critters either. Spending a sleepless night listening to a bear snuffling around outside your tent does not make for a relaxing camping trip! In fact, bears have become a greater danger in Ontario and can be quite ferocious in parts of Western Canada. Use preventive

measures: keep a clean campsite and hang your food in a distant tree, and you'll sleep soundly. Leave your campsite clean so the bears will not become a hazard for others in the area. Bears quickly learn to become effective campsite scavengers.

To store your food safely, find a tree that is at least rock-throwing distance from the door of your tent. The farther away it is from the camp the better. Select a strong limb about 12 feet (about 4 m) or higher from the ground. Tie a 30-foot (about 10 m) length of rope around a short, heavy stick or a rock. Throw this weight, with the rope attached, up and over the tree branch. It may take several tries to achieve this, but persevere.

Next, remove the stick, or rock, and loop the end of the rope through a sturdy strap on the food pack. Ask another camper to hold the pack high in the air, while you pull hard on the other end of the rope. This action will hoist the heavy pack up under the branch. With the length of rope in your hands, walk around the tree. Securely fasten the rope around the trunk of the tree. Try to position the food pack at least 5 feet (1.5 m) below the branch, and out from the trunk, or animals might still be able to reach the pack by climbing out on the branch.

Try to hang your food pack before nightfall. If you prefer to dine late, choose your tree early in the evening and throw the rope over an appropriate branch, ready for the food pack later. A final check for food debris before dark is a good habit that ensures that you haven't left anything around the camp that could attract animals. Never keep food in your tent.

HEAT EXHAUSTION

Heat exhaustion is a condition caused by prolonged exposure to heat, characterized by excessive sweating, faintness, dizziness, and, often, nausea. The first symptom of heat exhaustion is perspiration followed by a pale, clammy appearance. The person will feel weak and his or her skin will appear hot and flushed. Many people experience headaches from intense sunlight. Overheating is easily avoidable in areas where you can swim. If the current is too strong, cool your head by scooping water from the lake or river and pouring it over your head. Always wear a hat and sunglasses to reduce heat stroke. Prevent sunburn by using sunscreen with a high protection level and wearing a light long-sleeved cotton shirt during the peak hours of sunlight. Try to find a shady spot for your lunch break and stay out of the sun.

Gramma says, "Only mad dogs and Englishmen go out in the noon-day sun!"

HYPOTHERMIA

If it's a cold, wet day, be on the lookout for hypothermia symptoms when you stop for meals. Hypothermia is a dangerous condition wherein your body's core temperature drops so low that your body's defences begin to shut down. Be conscious of cooling down when you stop to take a break and especially if you suffer a chill by falling in the water or by getting soaked in a downfall of rain. This condition can occur more quickly if you are hungry and your blood sugar level is low. Try to keep moving to stay warm and perhaps eat a candy or drink some juice to tide you over until the meal is ready.

When the body experiences heat loss, muscles lose their strength and become cold and numb. Thoughts may be muddled and confused and short-term memory is affected. The first symptom is often prolonged shivering, which is the body's way of trying to produce heat.

The body's need for food increases greatly with the amount of physical exertion. Consequently, it is important to stop every one to two hours for a drink and a quick snack of trail mix or nuts. Stop more often if you are travelling with children or inexperienced canoeists. Also, in hot weather, stop more often and drink more frequently. In cold weather, eat lots of snacks and watch your group for symptoms of hypothermia such as lethargy and confusion.

For cold-weather trips, wool clothing will keep you warm even in wet weather. Unlike cotton, wool retains its insulating properties when wet. Always pack rainwear, including rain pants. Some rainwear isn't completely waterproof, but its insulating quality will keep you warmer than wearing shorts or sodden sweat pants. Drink a hot cup of tea or soup to warm up. Avoid alcohol when you are chilled.

Garbage

Unburnable garbage, such as cans, plastic containers, and aluminum foil, must be carried out of the park or camping area and deposited in a garbage facility. Remember to wash the cans before you flatten them to carry in your portable garbage bag because food scraps might attract animals. Unless you are staying in a campground with garbage facilities, you must bring a garbage bag or container and carry it throughout your entire trip. Hook it to the outside of your food pack at night and hang it with your food pack so that it won't attract animals. Leave a clean campsite for the next group of campers. Every camper plays an important role in preserving the wilderness.

Putting It All Together

Place all of your pots and utensils in an old cloth or plastic bag. When paddling, this "kitchen" bag will fit easily at the stern of the canoe and is not too awkward to manage on a portage as long as all your other belongings are neatly packed in large bags. After you have used the pots on an open fire, the outsides of the pots will turn black with soot and grease. This is one of the advantages of using a stove: your pots will stay relatively clean. Rather than scouring sooty pots, we recommend packing them separately and simply accepting the soot as something you must endure as a wilderness camper. If you are on a hiking trip, fit this bag of cooking equipment into a frame backpack or hook it on the outside. It will be too cumbersome to carry separately for long distances.

The grill and saw can be a nuisance to carry, especially with their sharp edges. If you are canoe tripping, however, you can strap them under a seat in the canoe. Make sure the grill is wrapped in an old cloth to save your skin from the sharp and sooty edges. Then place the small saw (with a guard on the blade) underneath the grill and strap it together with the grill under the canoe seat with bungie cords. Conveniently, the grill and saw can stay in this position while you portage the canoe.

If you are camping without a canoe, you may choose to leave the grill at home and instead use flat rocks in the fire pit to support the pot. You may also opt for a small axe or hatchet, instead of a saw, which can be strapped onto the outside of your food pack with a protective guard covering its blade.

Pack matches in two separate places to ensure that you have an adequate (and dry) supply. For example, place one supply in the first-aid kit in a ziplock bag and the other supply in a waterproof container in the food pack.

PACKING FOOD

When packing for a canoe trip, it is important to store all foods in waterproof, unbreakable containers. Always assume that there could be some water in the bottom of the canoe from rain, splashing from dogs boarding, or a slow leak in an old canoe. Line all your packs with plastic bags to keep the contents dry. Place your clothes in a garbage bag and squeeze all of the air out of the bag before twisting a twist-tie around the opening of the plastic bag. Be careful that the twist-tie doesn't puncture the plastic. The garbage bag should resemble a shrink-wrapped package. It is amazing how small your bundle of clothes will compress! Do the same with your sleeping bag.

If the pack accidentally falls in the water (when someone is getting in or out of the canoe or if the canoe tips over), the contents will remain dry if the pack is properly lined and it is immediately removed from the water. Taking care of any people who have capsized is obviously the most important issue, but once their safety is established, focus on retrieving your supplies. Try to get the pack out immediately for best results.

The following three tips will ensure that the inside of your food pack remains dry:

1) Place any food item that could melt or leak in a sealed container and then in a ziplock bag.

2) Before starting out, have your fresh fruits, vegetables, and cheese at room temperature. This will prevent condensation from forming inside the pack.

3) If you will be bringing some frozen items that will thaw during the day and then be used the first night, wrap them in double bags. Place them in your food pack but leave them outside of the sealed inner waterproof liner.

Preventing delicate foods from crushing is also an issue. Bread, fresh fruit, cookies, and squares are all foods that require special attention. We have included special packing suggestions to address this issue. By packing efficiently and labelling your meals clearly, you will reduce the chaos surrounding the dinner hour when everyone is hungry and you want to locate all of the ingredients quickly in order to get dinner started! This is why we assemble all of the ingredients for each dinner in separate, individual bags. You can quickly get the meal started and won't waste time rummaging through the food pack for each item.

Dry each vegetable separately and wrap separately to prevent spoilage. During hot weather, occasionally one of the vegetables may become mouldy if it is not dried sufficiently. By storing each vegetable separately, you will prevent the mould from spreading to the other vegetables. You will still be able to enjoy your meal, but it will have one less vegetable.

Pack the dehydrated dinners in the bottom of the food pack as crushing is not a concern and they will not be in the way when you access other items. Store supplies for breakfast, lunch, and snacks in the middle area, and keep more crushable items, such as bread and fresh produce, in the top part of the pack. If you have a pack with extra outside pockets, use the pockets to store items that are in plastic bottles, such as oil, pancake syrup, jam, and so on. Even though they are stored in leakproof containers and inside ziplock bags, there is always a risk of puncture. It is easier to clean up a messy outside pocket than the whole inside compartment of your food pack. Camping-supply stores offer a wide variety of dependable leakproof containers. They are worth the investment and can be reused for years. Ziplock bags can also be reused. Just ensure that they don't have a puncture.

Ziplock bags are also good for organizing different staples. Keep your cup-a-soup packages in one ziplock bag after removing all of the cardboard packaging. Do the same for instant oatmeal, hot chocolate, and so on. Keep bulk products in ziplock or heavy plastic bags with twist ties. Try to determine your group's needs as much as you can before packing. Before you pack, you will have to decide whether you will be having a pancake breakfast once or more often, and how many pots of oatmeal porridge you will plan to serve.

Throwaway plastic film containers are definitely worth saving. They seal well and hold up to 2 tablespoons (25 mL). They are great for garnishes and condiments, such as olives, vinegar, soy sauce, and salad dressing. Remember to put the film container in a baggie for extra assurance against leaking. Also consider using film containers for non-food items such as first-aid supplies, lotion, medication, or anything else that you require in small amounts.

PACKING COOKIES AND BARS — SNACK PACKS

Save small milk cartons, individual-sized cereal boxes, or other fairly heavy cardboard boxes of about that size. Stack cookies or bars in a number likely needed for serving. Wrap the cookies or bars in plastic bags and place them inside the milk carton or box. If there is extra space, cut the carton down the middle and compress it until it is the right size. Neatly fold over the tops by cutting them down to the level of the cookies/bars. Tape around the sides and over the ends with masking tape.

You will end up with a small package of snacks that will be quite sturdy and won't be crushed in your food pack. We call these "snack packs." Make several "snack packs" for midday breaks or dessert. Try to use the entire packet in one sitting, rather than repackaging the leftovers for another time. Use the cardboard packaging to help start your next campfire.

STAPLES

Before we start packing, we make a detailed checklist of everything we'll need in our staple supply. Checklists of these supplies are provided on page 42. The first set of items suggest what you will most likely need for your breakfasts and lunches, and for your drinks and snacks. The quantities given are for four people. To calculate what you will need for your trip, simply multiply the amounts given by the number of days or uses for each item. (For example, oatmeal for four people times two breakfasts.)

The sub-section we call *Staples* is more like your "portable pantry." These are items that have multiple applications — all-purpose flour, brown and white sugar, salt and pepper, milk powder. The amounts listed in these sections are approximate, since there are many different uses for them. For example, you may require oil for greasing the frying pan, preparing pancakes for two breakfasts, and to add to one or two dinner recipes. Since a single container of oil is easier to carry than several small containers, it makes more sense to calculate the amount of oil you'll need and carry it in one container. We have based these quantities on a six-day trip for four people. You can adjust these quantities according to what you will need for the duration of your trip, and depending on which recipes you choose to make.

Your emergency rations should include items from all these lists. We usually include soup, oatmeal, hot chocolate, and drink crystals.

Except for the staple requirements, a checklist for your dinners is not included here. We strongly recommend that you pre-package your dinner ingredients and put all the ingredients for each recipe in one large plastic bag along with the cooking instructions — all ingredients, that is, except the staple ingredients. All your oil requirements, for example, will be calculated in advance and added to your portable pantry supply. When you are at the camp-site, the key ingredients you will need for each dinner will be in a labelled package, one package for each dinner. Clearly labelled packages take the guesswork out of meal preparation. Once you have planned your dinner menus for your trip (see *Suggested Meal Plans*, page *141*), refer to each recipe for the ingredients and the packing instructions.

BREAKFAST ITEMS:

- *Authentic Oatmeal Porridge:* 1½ cups (375 mL) quick-cooking oatmeal for one breakfast for 4 people (see page *55*).
- *Cold cereal, muesli, or granola*: Take enough for your group.
- *Compote:* 1½ cups (375 mL) dried fruit for one breakfast for 4 people (see page *66*).
- *Cream of Wheat:* ¾ cup (175 mL) cream of wheat for one break-fast for 4 people (see page *60*).
- *Instant hot cereal:* 1 to 2 commercially prepared packages per person per breakfast, plus extra for emergency supplies.
- *Make-Your-Own Instant Oatmeal:* One breakfast for 4 people (see page *56*).
- *Muffin mix:* 2 cups (500 mL) of mix makes 4 generous muffins.
- *Pancake mix:* 2½ cups (625 mL) for one breakfast for 4 people.
- *Wholesome Pancakes:* One breakfast for 4 people (see page *63*).

LUNCH ITEMS:

- *Bread:* 2 to 3 slices per person for lunch, plus extra for toast with breakfast and to accompany dinner if desired.
  1) Sliced rye bread is dense enough to travel fairly well in the food pack. It will stay fresh for three to four days depending on

weather conditions. Keep it well sealed between uses so that it doesn't dry out.

2) Sliced, shrink-wrapped packages of rye, pumpernickel, linseed, etc. will pack well and can be used for five to six days (or more depending on the weather). They come in 1 lb (454 g) packages and usually 1 package will be enough for 4 to 6 servings (or one lunch).

Note: Buy shrink-wrapped bread fresh just before you leave. Do not buy it early and freeze. This type of bread can turn very crumbly if it is frozen and then thawed.

3) Pita bread will keep for three to four days and adds variety to the other heavy bread options.

4) Bagels will keep for three to four days and are excellent served with cream cheese and cucumber.

5) Dried Italian bread called "fresne" (or "fresine") is best packed in a rigid container as it is rather brittle. This bread is available in Italian grocery stores. Leave it in the bottom of the food pack until you have eaten the rest of your bread products. Rehydrate as needed by dipping the dried slices very quickly in *treated* water or just sprinkling with treated water. Set out to rehydrate and after a few minutes it becomes a great chewy sandwich bread. It is a bit bulky, but an excellent product.

Note: Always use *treated* water to rehydrate the bread.

- *Cheese:* Bring 1 small sealed block of cheese (8 oz/227 g) per day for lunch. Once opened, plan to finish at that meal. It becomes oily and difficult to repack after opening. Lots of varieties are available: old cheddar, havarti, colby, etc. Cream cheese keeps for two to three days and makes a good sandwich with cucumber for lunch. Some varieties come in 250-mL plastic resealable containers. A block of parmesan will keep well for long trips of up to twenty days, but remember to pack a grater. A small amount of grated parmesan adds a lot of flavour.
- *Fresh fruit and vegetables:* A suggested amount of fresh produce for a seven-day outing could be one 2-lb (907-g) bag of carrots

(8 or 10) and 2 small cucumbers and 8 apples.

Fresh produce is usually used at lunch. Slice a cucumber to enjoy with your bread, cheese, and soup. Or share a piece of fruit with some cookies and hot chocolate after dinner. Choose firm fruits and vegetables such as cucumbers and carrots and apples and pears. Select small cucumbers so that you can use a whole cucumber in one lunch, rather than risking spoilage. Plan to eat fruits and cucumbers in the first three or four days as they bruise more easily than carrots, which keep the longest. Fresh produce is a treasured treat! For backpacking trips where it is even more important to reduce your load, you might have to limit the fresh produce to half a serving per person per day.

- *Instant soup:* Bring 1 family-size package (4 servings) per day, plus some extra for emergency rations.

DRINKS:

- *Coffee:* ½ cup (125 mL) per serving for 4 people (see page *48*).
- *Drink crystals:* Take enough to make 6 to 8 cups (1.5 to 2 L) of juice per person per day. It is important to drink lots of liquid, especially if you are exercising vigorously in hot weather (see *Heat Exhaustion,* page *36*). Bring a variety of flavours of drink crystals and add some to your *treated* water. It is probably easier to have two smaller drinking bottles so that you'll have one bottle in each canoe and two different flavours to choose from. Although many people wouldn't usually drink this stuff at home, on the trail most of us get a kick out of deciding whether to have "passion fruit," "lemon-lime," or iced tea. When one container is empty, you can purify a fresh batch of water since this process takes at least 10 minutes. This way you will always have something on hand to drink. Bring a few extra packages of drink crystals.
- *Hot chocolate:* Buy instant individual packages or bulk powder. Bring extra for your emergency supplies.
- *Tea:* Bring enough to make three times per day or less if your group doesn't drink tea. Try to determine the number of tea bags required and then toss in a few extras. For variety, bring herbal teas such as peppermint and camomile. Tea can be made in a small cook pot (see page *49*).

SNACKS:

- *Cookies and bars:* Bring one "snack pack" per day plus a few extra (for packing instructions see page *41*).

- *Dried soy beans and dried green peas:* These are available at bulk food stores.
- *Hard candy:* Individually wrapped candies are easy to carry in your pocket for a quick energy burst when you are ready for lunch but your group decides to paddle for another half hour.
- *Nuts:* Choose from a wide variety. Nuts provide lots of calories when you are exercising and are compact to carry. Nuts can also be heavy in large amounts, however, so consider mixing them with other lighter ingredients to make a trail mix.
- *Trail mix:* There are many varieties available; your choice will be based on your group's preferences. You can also make your own. Adding cereal can be economical, but it also adds bulk. Kids and chocolate lovers will enjoy the addition of M&Ms™ or Smarties™ to the trail mix — the candy coating prevents the chocolate centres from melting. Most trail mixes consist of a combination of nuts, seeds, and dried fruit.

STAPLES:

The amounts of the ingredients on the following list are based roughly on a six-day trip for four people. Where an amount is not suggested, pack according to your own needs.
- *All-purpose flour:* ½ cup (125 mL).
- *Brown sugar:* ½ cup (125 mL) for adding to porridge (or more depending on your group's tastes).
- *Cinnamon:* 1 to 2 tbsp (15 to 25 mL) to add to porridge or muffins.
- *Condiments:* Individually wrapped mustard, relish, ketchup, soy sauce, tartar sauce, horseradish, and lemon juice packets are ideal. Save your leftover packets from fast-food restaurants. For longer trips, fill leakproof containers with condiments of your choice. Dijon mustard, spicy salsa, and flavoured oils are a few ways to add flavour without adding much weight to your food pack. Several experienced canoe trippers have told us that gourmet condiments improve everyone's enjoyment of campfire meals immeasurably.

Flour can be used to thicken sauces if they are too watery. In a cup, gradually add ⅓ cup (75 mL) cold water to 1 to 2 tbsp (15 to 25 mL) all-purpose flour. Stir to make a paste. Add some of the hot liquid from your dinner. Stir and then pour this flour mixture into the pot. Stir and cook for a few minutes until thick. Serve soon or the flour may cause the food to burn the bottom of the pot.

- *Garlic:* Fresh or powdered garlic will work equally well. If you prefer to take fresh garlic, just slice it in with rehydrating vegetables; if you take a powdered equivalent, add it in with the other spices in the recipe. See individual recipes for detailed packing and "At Campsite" instructions.
- *Honey:* ½ cup (125 mL) for breakfast, lunch, and snacks.
- *Jam:* 1 cup (250 mL) for using at breakfast or lunch, or for serving with muffins. Pack in a leakproof container and put it inside a ziplock bag.
- *Marshmallows:* 15 to 20 marshmallows will be adequate but bring more if children are coming. Carry them in a ziplock bag. Toast on a stick for a campfire dessert, or add to a cup of hot chocolate. During hot weather, however, marshmallows can become very gooey.
- *Milk powder:* 1 cup (250 mL). Add to porridge while cooking, or mix as directed and pour over cereal. You may need more if your companions use milk in their tea or coffee.
- *Muffin mix or biscuit mix:* 2 cups (500 mL) for 4 to 6 large muffins or biscuits for one meal. If you plan to eat muffins or biscuits more often, double or triple the amount as required. If you plan to have dumplings for a dinner, pack the mix with that dinner as instructed. Biscuit mix also works well for scones, dumplings, and corn bread (see *Biscuits,* page *120*).
- *Oil:* 1½ cups (375 mL). This amount depends on how often you need oil for dinner preparations (see packing list given with recipe) as well as the number of pancake breakfasts you plan to have. Store in a leakproof container and keep it inside a ziplock bag.
- *Peanut butter:* 1 cup (250 mL). Carry in an unbreakable plastic container that is stored inside a ziplock bag for double protection. Use for breakfast, lunch, and possibly for a snack. If you plan to use peanut butter in one of the dinners, you will need to bring more.
- *Potato flakes:* 1 cup (250 mL) for thickening soups or dinners.
- *Salt and pepper:* Ensure they are in small, plastic, leakproof shakers.
- *Syrup:* 1 cup (250 mL) for each pancake breakfast.
- *White sugar:* about 1 cup (250 mL) or 1½ cups (375 mL) for use in coffee and tea.
- *Raisins:* 1 cup (250 mL) for porridge or muffins. Increase amount if desired for a snack food.
- *Sterilized milk:* This is available in 250-mL or 1-L sizes. It does not require refrigeration until after opening, but is heavy and

bulky to carry. Children who don't like powdered milk might enjoy this compromise to fresh milk. Sterilized half-and-half cream is also available in 250-mL containers.

- *Tofu:* This is an excellent protein booster and adds texture and heartiness to vegetarian meals. Silken tofu, which is packaged in special sealed boxes and does not require refrigeration until after opening, is an ideal choice for trips that are longer than two days.

WATER

Bring fresh water or juice from home to start off your trip then use treated water for the duration of your trip. Always treat water even when it looks clean. Take precautions!

Drinking water must be *treated* by one of the following methods:

1) boiling for five minutes,
2) dissolving water-purification tablets in it and waiting 10 minutes before drinking, or
3) filtering with a water-purification system.

Note: People with a thyroid condition should not use iodine tablets.

Giardiasis is a disease that can be transmitted to humans by drinking water contaminated with animal or human excrement, which carries the protozoan *Giardia lamblia.* Giardiasis can cause very unpleasant digestive symptoms and must be treated with antibiotics to kill the protozoan. If water will be boiled for 5 minutes during cooking it is not necessary to treat it first. When you prepare your drinking water at the campsite, make sure you have enough for your cooking needs.

> I contracted this nasty parasite while travelling through Pakistan. I treated the disease with three different antibiotics before finally killing it six months later — definitely worth avoiding! — *Jill*

COFFEE AND TEA

When planning a trip and determining your supplies, you should ask everyone:

1) if they drink coffee and tea
2) if they take milk, cream, and sugar and
3) if they prefer regular or decaffeinated tea or coffee.

People have definite preferences in this area, but some compromising may be necessary to facilitate the packing and carrying.

COFFEE

Preparing and enjoying camp coffee is a memorable event. Years later, many campers will fondly recall sitting at a particularly beautiful spot quietly enjoying the surroundings "with a cup of great coffee."

Good camp coffee, like coffee at home, requires both good water and good coffee. How you make coffee will be determined by your equipment. Some people may choose to carry a coffee pot — usually a percolator or a drip pot. An easier alternative is a simple plastic cone filter-holder; these come in various sizes and cost only a few dollars. Be sure to bring the right size of filters and don't overfill the filters with coffee, lest they clog up.

If you are using a cook pot for making coffee, choose the size according to the number of cups of coffee being made. Measure cold water into the pot. Add 1 tbsp (15 mL) ground coffee for each cup of water and 1 tbsp (15 mL) coffee "for the pot." Cover, bring to the boil, and immediately move the pot to the edge of the fire to allow it to simmer gently for 8 minutes, or reduce the heat on the campstove. Remove the pot from the heat for a minute so that the grounds will settle to the bottom. Serve carefully, leaving the sludge in the bottom of the pot.

If you are making coffee for four people, keep in mind that most people like to drink at least one large mug of coffee. Start out with 7 cups (1.75 L) of water and 8 tbsp — or ½ cup (125 mL) — of coffee. This ensures that everyone will receive a generous amount.

Instant coffee is an easier option, but many people are not satisfied with the flavour. However, instant coffee is handy if there is only one coffee drinker in the group.

Last summer, Daryn was finally invited on a canoe trip with us. He was really excited about the food after hearing so many stories about the wonderful wilderness meals. By day two of the trip, however, Daryn had a terrible headache. On day three, he looked at the label of the coffee and discovered the source of his headaches — decaffeinated coffee. Oops! Luckily the food was so good that he was forgiving.   – Jill

Using coffee filter bags is another good way of making coffee for a group. Use a small pot to brew the filter bags. Boil 4 to 6 cups (1 to 1.5 L) water, add the filter bag, and let the coffee simmer for 6 to 8 minutes.

TEA

Boil 4 to 6 cups (1 L to 1.5 L) of water in a small pot. Add 1 to 2 tea bags to the boiling water and remove the pot from the heat. Put the lid on the pot and let the tea sit for 3 to 4 minutes. Serve. The tea will cool very quickly in the metal pot.

Cream

Cream is available in individual creamers, but it is only possible to use these for short trips. Half-and-half cream is also available in 250-mL containers.

Milk

Sterilized milk and sterilized half-and-half cream come in 250-mL or 1-L boxes.

Milk and cream are bulky and heavy to carry. If you don't use up the contents of a container after serving, it won't be convenient to carry the remainder in the opened container. You can transfer the milk into a leakproof container and carry the leftover portion for a short period of time, until the next break for tea or coffee. Otherwise, choose a size that could be used at one meal. For example, the 1-L size could be all used up at breakfast: on cereal, to drink, and in coffee/tea. Any leftover milk can replace water in the pancake mix.

Milk powder is easy to carry and rehydrate. The ratio is ⅓ cup (75 mL) milk powder to 1 cup (250 mL) *treated* water.

Sugar

This should be with your staple foods. Carry extra if people in your group use it in their tea or coffee.

Have a Great Trip!

Food is closely linked with morale on outdoor adventure trips. Because you are expending so much energy, your appetite will inevitably be large. Regular meals with snacks in the mid-morning and mid-afternoon keep spirits high while you push your body beyond its usual level of exertion. Train yourself to drink often to prevent dehydration and keep yourself feeling energized. Even if the weather is rainy or cold, good food will warm your tummy, give you energy, and keep a smile on your face.

At the end of each trip, look at what you have brought home in the food pack and assess whether you overpacked or underpacked, and which foods were most popular. Much will depend on the weather, the level of activity, and appetites of your group. Use this knowledge to improve meal planning and packing for your next trip. Record new ideas for one-pot meals or unique serving suggestions. Every trip is a different experience and, when it comes to food, there are always new discoveries.

The river seems far away now as we motor along Highway 69. We pass gas stations, snack bars, and marinas. Billboards advertising resorts and country dining pop up around every rock outcrop. We can feel the humidity rising as we drive south.

Just a short time ago, we remember dipping our paddles in the river, drawing back until our muscles ached and then lifting and pulling again. The sunlight sparkled on the rippling water all around us. We were entertained by a heron, a loon, and a huge flock of turkey vultures blackening the shoreline in a feeding frenzy.

We recall the last swim — alone in the early morning, surrounded by silvery mist. There was sadness as we broke camp on our last morning knowing we wouldn't return until next summer. The fall colours that have deepened since we started out last week remind us that the season is ending. We've collected some of the brightest leaves to take home as mementoes.

Sun-baked and fuzzy-headed, we travel homeward — back to the "real world." We wonder what we'll make for dinner when we get home. It probably won't be as delicious as the wholesome meals we've enjoyed over the last week!

Driving home, we treasure the memories of another wilderness adventure.   *– Jill*

RECIPES

BREAKFAST

When you have a long day of paddling ahead of you, you need a quick and substantial breakfast that will sustain you throughout the morning. The fastest, easiest camp-style breakfast is hot cereal. Try other recipes for variety and save the elaborate ones for lazy mornings when you aren't in a hurry.

AUTHENTIC OATMEAL PORRIDGE

It is worth the extra time to prepare your own nutritious porridge. Don't worry about cleaning a messy pot. Pour some water into the pot after serving the porridge and let it soak while you enjoy breakfast. Serves 4.

- Add 1½ cups (375 mL) quick-cooking rolled oats to 3½ cups (875 mL) boiling water in a pot. Add ½ tsp (2 mL) salt as desired.
- Stir and cook for 3 to 5 minutes.
- Serve with powdered milk, or as is.

SERVING OPTIONS:
- Add coconut or raisins and cinnamon to the boiling water for a delicious change.
- Add blueberries or other wild berries to the cooked cereal.
- For a tropical taste, add sliced banana and coconut.

Young children might enjoy *Peanut Crunch Squares* (see page *139*) or *Marshmallow Crispy Squares* (see page *138*) for a quick-energy breakfast.

Make-Your-Own Instant Oatmeal

This is a healthful, low-salt, low-sugar alternative to commercially prepared instant hot cereal. Make the mix at home. Serves 4.

1½ cups (375 mL) quick-cooking rolled oats
½ cup (125 mL) milk powder
¼ cup (50 mL) wheat germ
2 tbsp (25 mL) brown sugar
1 tsp (5 mL) cinnamon
½ tsp (2 mL) salt, as desired

AT HOME:
- Blend about ½ cup (125 mL) of the quick-cooking rolled oats in a blender to make a fine flour-like product. This will give the prepared oatmeal a more creamy texture.
- Toast the remaining 1 cup (250 mL) oatmeal at 375°F (190°C) on a baking sheet in the oven. Watch carefully and stir once or twice until the oatmeal is slightly browned — about 5 to 10 minutes. Cool.
- Combine the quick-cooking oats (blended and toasted portions), milk powder, wheat germ, brown sugar, cinnamon, and salt (if desired).

PACK:
Oatmeal mixture in a ziplock bag.

AT CAMPSITE:
- Put about ½ cup (125 mL) of the mix into your mug and add about ½ cup (125 mL) boiling water. Stir until thickened. Add more water if necessary.

SERVING OPTIONS:
- Add fresh fruit (blueberries, banana) or dried fruit (apples, peaches, raisins).
- Add milk.

VARIATIONS:
Add sunflower or poppy seeds, nuts, or dried fruit to the recipe, as desired. You can create your own version from this basic recipe.

INSTANT HOT CEREAL

This commercial product is a favourite for quick breakfasts and is very convenient.

Allow 1½ to 2 packets per person per breakfast.

• Pour the contents of the package into your cup and add boiling water.
• Stir until thickened and enjoy.

SERVING OPTIONS:
- Add dried fruit or fresh berries.
- Add milk powder or make the porridge thinner and eat it without milk. Serve it in your cup after finishing your tea or coffee.

CREAMY COUSCOUS

*With a consistency similar to rice pudding, this delicious breakfast
is amazingly quick to prepare and will sustain you for several hours.*

1 cup (250 mL) prunes
1 cup (250 mL) couscous
¾ cup (175 mL) milk powder
⅓ cup (75 mL) brown sugar
1 tsp (5 mL) cinnamon
2 tsp (10 mL) dried butter flavouring

PACK:
Prunes in a plastic bag.
Couscous in a plastic bag.
All other ingredients in a ziplock bag.
Wrap all of the ingredients in a labelled, heavy plastic bag, with
   "At Campsite" instructions inside.

AT CAMPSITE:
• Boil 4 cups (1 L) water in large pot.
• Add prunes to boiling water and cook for 5 minutes.
• Mix ½ cup (125 mL) cold water with the milk powder, brown
   sugar, cinnamon, and butter flavouring in a ziplock bag.
• Add the milk mixture to the cooked prunes, stirring constantly.
• Add couscous and stir to combine.
• Remove from heat and let stand for 5 minutes.
• Stir to blend and serve.

SERVING OPTIONS:
- Add jam or syrup.

VARIATIONS:

Instead of the prunes, substitute any of the following:

1) Banana: add ½ cup (125 mL) banana chips.
2) Banana/chocolate: add ½ cup (125 mL) banana chips and 1 tbsp (15 mL) cocoa powder.
3) Peanut butter: add ½ cup (125 mL) peanut butter.

If you carry the ingredients with your staples, you can make this dish quickly to fill out another meal after a particularly strenuous day. It also makes an excellent dessert and can be used as an emergency ration.

CREAM OF WHEAT

High in iron, this hot cereal is a light-tasting alternative to porridge.

4 cups (1 L) water
¾ cup (175 mL) quick-cooking cream of wheat

• Boil the water and add the cream of wheat. Stir and cook for 3 minutes.

SERVING OPTIONS:
- Add chopped dates, raisins, cinnamon, or sliced banana.
- If you have blueberry sauce left over from last night's dinner, you can use it to embellish various breakfasts. (Remember to store the leftover sauce in a plastic container in the food pack overnight.)

EGGS

If you are craving an omelette or scrambled eggs, break raw eggs into a small leakproof container — they can be carried safely for one to two days. Alternatively, Egg Beaters™ is a frozen, commercially available egg product that should keep for a few days without refrigeration if the container is kept sealed. You might consider using this product in the early days of your trip. Powdered egg can be used in baking, but we don't recommend it for breakfast as it lacks the texture and flavour of real eggs.

Tofu scrambler, a scrambled-egg substitute, can be easily prepared with a commercial tofu scrambler mix and silken tofu, which doesn't require refrigeration until opened. This could be used as a hearty breakfast item, served with toast, or as a sandwich filling for lunch.

Cold Cereal, Muesli, or Granola

Cold cereal is bulky; granola and muesli are heavy. However, you might want to bring cereal if children are coming and they are especially fond of cereal for breakfast. Serve with sterilized milk or powdered milk. Top with fresh berries if they are available around your campsite.

Children will enjoy looking for blueberries while you prepare breakfast. Just make sure that they know exactly what type of berries to pick. The blue-coloured berries from juniper bushes can look very similar to blueberries, but will cause a bad stomach ache if eaten. The foliage of juniper bushes is very different from blueberry bushes, however, so blueberries should be easy to identify. When in doubt, an adult should accompany children for berry picking.

When I was trekking on the Juan de Fuca Strait Marine Trail on Vancouver Island, there were mounds of blue bear scat all over the trail. It was salal berry season. Once Daryn and I saw a scrape on a tree with a distinct outline of claws in a downward swoop revealing the wood beneath the injured bark. We were on edge for at least half an hour. The last thing I wanted to happen was to surprise a bear, so we sang and clapped our way along the trail, especially at points where we couldn't see around a bend.   *– Jill*

Basic rule for camping in bear territory: If you see a black bear, make noise. If you see a brown bear, play dead.

PANCAKES AND SYRUP (EASY VERSION)

This recipe uses a commercial mix, but don't be put off — pancakes cooked on a campfire always taste great!

- Mix 2½ cups (625 mL) pancake mix with water, according to the directions on the package. (Add ½ to 1 cup/125 to 250 mL fresh berries if they are available at your campsite.)
- Oil the frying pan and place it on the grill.
- Drop the batter by spoonfuls onto the hot pan. (Sometimes it is easier to make one large pancake that is the same size as the pan.)
- Flip the pancakes when bubbles have formed on the surface and cook for another minute.
- Serve golden brown with syrup, honey, jam, or sliced banana.
- If you make too much pancake batter, cook it all into pancakes anyway and keep the extra pancakes for a mid-morning snack with jam.

BLUEBERRY SAUCE

If you pick blueberries, prepare your sauce using 2 parts blueberries to 1 part water. For example, add 1 cup (250 mL) blueberries to ½ cup water (125 mL) and about ¼ cup (50 mL) sugar, or to taste. Bring to the boil in a small pot and cook for 4 to 5 minutes. Serve hot over pancakes.

We often plan our wilderness outings to coincide with wild-blueberry season. Blueberries are delicious when freshly picked and eaten immediately or collected to enhance breakfast, lunch, or dessert. We add them to almost every meal if we time it right and they are plentiful. Once we had blueberry pancakes with blueberry sauce — doubly decadent!

WHOLESOME PANCAKES

Made from scratch, these pancakes live up to their name. Make this mix at home. It makes a generous amount for 4 people.

1 ¼ cups (300 mL) all-purpose flour
1 cup (250 mL) whole wheat flour
½ cup (125 mL) yellow cornmeal
* ⅓ cup (75 mL) powdered buttermilk
* 2 tbsp (25 mL) powdered egg
1 tbsp (15 mL) sugar
1 tbsp (15 mL) baking powder
½ tsp (2 mL) salt
3 tbsp (45 mL) oil
Available at bulk-food stores.

AT HOME:
• Mix all of the ingredients except the oil in a large ziplock bag.

AT CAMPSITE:
• Add the oil and about 2½ cups (625 mL) water to the dried ingredients in the ziplock bag.
• Close the bag and knead to make a thin batter. Add a little more water if necessary. This is the easiest way to mix the batter and also to pour it out when you fry the pancakes.
• Oil the frying pan and fry the pancakes.
• Flip the pancakes after bubbles have formed on their surface and cook for another minute.
• Serve golden brown with syrup, honey, or jam.

VARIATION:
- Add ½ cup (125 mL) fresh or dried berries to the pancake batter.

MUFFINS

Vary the muffins by adding raisins, currants, cinnamon, or fresh berries to the basic mix.

- Mix 2 cups (500 mL) commercially prepared muffin mix with water according to the directions on the package. Do not over-mix. Add options: cinnamon, raisins, currants, or ½ cup (125 mL) to 1 cup (250 mL) fresh berries if available.
- Oil the inside of the pot lid (or frying pan).
- Drop the muffin dough in 4 or 6 mounds.
- Put the clean, dry large cook pot upside down over the lid (or frying pan) to create an oven.
- Set on the grill about 6" (15 cm) from the bed of coals.
- Bake for 15 to 20 minutes.
- Serve with jam or honey.

If muffins do not appear to be cooked on the tops and are burning on the bottoms, remove them from the pan and set them out on a plate. Quickly re-oil the pan and turn the muffins back into the pan, upside down. Resume cooking for another 5 minutes or so. This is not a gourmet method, but it will save your muffins and they will still taste great.

Muffins bake better over a bed of coals, so plan to make them on a day when you are planning a slow, leisurely breakfast. If you are baking with a campstove, a heat diffuser can give more even heat distribution over the bottom of the frying pan.

Toast and Jam/Peanut Butter

You can open a package of bread that you intend to finish at lunch and use a couple of pieces for toast. If everyone in your group likes toast for breakfast, you'll have to take along extra bread. Use a long-handled fork or a forked stick to toast the bread. You can also toast it directly on the grill.

Biscuits with Jam

Fresh hot bread is always a welcome treat on our wilderness trips. Biscuits can complement your dinner or, served with jam, make a delicious breakfast alternative. Add blueberries, cheese, or cornmeal to a basic biscuit mix, depending on your group's preferences. For recipe see page *120*.

COMPOTE (STEWED FRUIT)

This can be made from any combination of dried fruit, such as prunes, apricots, apples, pears, and peaches.

- Put about 1½ cups (375 mL) dried fruit into a small pot with about 3 cups (750 mL) water.
- Bring to the boil and simmer with the lid on for 5 to 10 minutes.
- Serve hot or allow to cool.

SERVING OPTION:
- Serve as a topping over hot cereal.

Dried apricots, apple, and prunes can be prepared the night before at the campsite to be ready for breakfast the next day. If you make it the night before, transfer the stewed fruit into a sealed container and store it in the food pack.

Chum, Mom, and I discovered fruit compote served over oatmeal porridge while touring around Scotland. We preferred this to the typical "fried" Scottish breakfast.
— *Bonnie*

LUNCH

On sultry summer days, lunch is the ideal time to take an extended break and go for a refreshing dip in the water. To simplify preparation and clean-up, we recommend using your campstove for preparing lunch on the trail. Lunch usually evolves around variations on the basic soup-and-sandwich theme. You'll be surprised at how savoury instant soup can be — even on sweltering days. We've also welcomed soup on blustery fall days and drizzling grey days in the summer. Whatever the weather conditions, you'll enjoy these no-fuss lunches that provide energy to keep your muscles working through the afternoon.

Lunch Suggestions

Choose a selection from the following choices:

BREAD:
- rye bread, sliced
- pumpernickel/linseed/rye bread/flax seed/sunflower seed, and so on (any sliced and shrink-wrapped, heavy variety)
- bagels
- pita bread
- rice cakes (bulky but lightweight)
- fresne (or "fresine") bread for last days of trip

VEGGIES:
- raw veggies (carrots, celery, cucumber)

SOUP:
- instant soup (quick and easy for lunch)
- See *Types of Soup*, page 70.

SANDWICH FILLINGS:
- cheese
- cream cheese
- hummus (lasts for 2 to 3 days)
- peanut butter/jam/honey
- cashew or almond butter, or tahini
- hard-boiled eggs (last for 2 to 3 days)

FRUIT:
- dried fruits (apricots, apple, papaya, raisins, etc.)
- fresh fruits (apples, firm pears)

COOKIES AND BARS:
- See *Desserts and Snacks*, page 124

DRINKS:
- tea/coffee/juice

MEAT OPTIONS:
- sardines, oysters (in cans)
- summer sausage (buy the cloth-bag variety and slice it as you use it to prevent it from drying out)
- pepperoni, beef jerky

We've heard stories from people who have gone on guided canoe trips and were disappointed to discover that "lunch" consisted of just a few handfuls of trail mix. Considering the amount of energy you are expending, you'll find that even people who typically skip lunch will experience hunger pangs and want to eat a balanced meal, even if it is just a small one. Others prefer to keep paddling and not take time out for a leisurely lunch.

Our lunch suggestions are not time-consuming, and if you are in a big hurry, you can skip the soup and just make sandwiches with bread, cheese, and a bit of sliced cucumber. Stopping for half an hour to do this will make your journey much more pleasant and the dispositions of the people in your group will be much improved. Having enough food at regular intervals is important to sustain everyone. Soup is good in hot and cold weather and works well with plain bread and cheese. It also provides good nourishment and fluids.

If you are travelling in a small party, you can be much more flexible about mealtimes than you can in a larger group. Stopping for breaks and lunch takes longer if your group is larger. Ask the members of your group if they usually eat lunch and make a decision before you leave. Our unanimous recommendation: "Don't skip lunch!"

KID-FRIENDLY TIPS

You can make camp food more fun for kids with these suggestions:
- carrots or apple slices dipped in peanut butter
- rice cakes (available in many flavours)
- peanut-butter-and-honey sandwich spread (½ peanut butter, ½ honey)

- honey-butter sandwich spread (½ honey, ½ butter or margarine)
- make-your-own sandwich creation: let your kids go crazy! The "no-rule" sandwich is always a great hit with kids. Give them a selection of foods from which to choose, monitoring them so that they don't waste food. They can add trail mix, ketchup, cheese, jam, cinnamon, or raisins. You can even let kids concoct their own special "swamp water" juice mixture. Mix half of one type of drink crystal with half of another package and see what flavour (and colour) ensues. The more gruesome and swamp-like the colour, the better.

TYPES OF SOUP

1) CUP-A-SOUP — individual servings
Everyone can choose a soup flavour and add the powder to her or his cup. Fill each cup with boiling water. Stir and serve according to the directions on the package.

Individual servings are bulkier because there is more packaging. For couples travelling together, individual packets can work well, but for larger groups, we recommend family-sized packages.

Instant individual packets can provide a greater variety of meals. As well as soup, beans and rice, chili, jambalaya, and curry are available.

To save space and reduce garbage, buy the kind that is packaged in a paper sleeve, not a wax-coated cup.

2) INSTANT SOUP — family sized
Add the contents of the package to water and bring to the boil. Cook for 3 to 5 minutes, according to the directions on the package.
Note: Some packaged soups require 20 minutes of cooking. Read the instructions before purchasing, especially if you don't want to take this extra time to prepare the soup. Also, experiment with different brands to find the kind you like best. Some brands are less salty than others.

HAPPY HOUR

While camping in the backwoods, wine and beer are not at all practical for a before-dinner drink. They are in breakable glass containers; they are bulky and heavy. You won't have to visit too many campsites before discovering that some people don't treat the environment with respect. Shards of glass and bottle caps littering the campsite are an eyesore and a hazard in the pristine wilderness.

Here are some suggestions for beverages that will stimulate an evening of heart-to-heart discussions and whet your appetites for supper:

- boxed wine (first night out)
- rum with drink crystals — peach, lemonade, orange, apple, cranberry, and so on
- tea 'n' rum
- coffee with brandy
- scotch (neat)
- tea/coffee/juice

Carry alcohol in a sturdy plastic vessel. Avoid carrying glass containers. Always put safety first and drink moderately. You can enjoy a relaxing happy hour while watching the sunset as your dinner simmers.

> One year, my brother Max and I bought Mom a plastic rum flask for canoe trips. It turned out to be less sturdy than we thought, however. When the pack hit the ground too hard, the flask split open — spilling its contents all over her sleeping bag. Mom regretted the lost happy hours, but enjoyed the lingering fumes at bedtime.
>
> – Jill

DINNER

An average appetite can swell to gargantuan proportions after an active day on the trail. Try to time your schedule so that you don't have to cook in the dark. Stop early enough to give yourself ample time to set up your tent, change your clothes, search for firewood, select a tree to hang the food pack in, and — finally! — prepare dinner. Delegating tasks among your group will mean more free time for everyone later in the evening.

The *Dinner* section is organized into *Basic Dinners, First-Night-Out Dinners*, and *Quick Dinners. Basic Dinner* recipes make use of dehydrated foods that are rehydrated at the campsite. *First-Night-Out Dinners* tend to be more perishable, bulky, and sometimes heavy. On the first night on the trail, dinner doesn't have to follow many of the campfire meal criteria because you won't be carrying or storing it for long. *Quick Dinners* are for campers who want to eat right away, instead of enjoying some quiet time before dinner, and can be quickly prepared at the campsite.

All of the dinner recipes included in this book are designed to serve four hungry campers. Most of these recipes can be stretched to feed six people by using the old "add-a-cup-of-water-to-the-pot" technique. Just prepare more of the starch (i.e., rice or pasta) and add more liquid to the pot. When preparing the dried vegetables at home, just add a few more of some of the vegetables; for example, four carrots instead of three, or two onions instead of one. By plumping up the recipes in this way you can easily modify the amount to feed everyone. For larger groups, double or triple the recipes as necessary.

The dinner recipes are all complete and do not require additional side dishes to make the meals well rounded and substantial. We are sure you'll be satisfied with the dinners as suggested. We seldom consider any additions to the meals — not even sliced bread. And dessert, when served, is usually later in the evening because we are too full to eat it immediately after dinner.

Many of the dinner recipes offer variations, allowing you to alter the recipes to provide more options and to please different tastes. The seasonings can be modified easily to suit your preferences. If someone in your group doesn't like a certain vegetable, just substitute something else of your choice. All of the recipes are flexible and include a large variety of vegetables for visual interest, flavour, and good nutrition. In addition, each meal contains lots of carbohydrates and protein to provide your body with nutrition and sustained energy.

BASIC DINNERS

All of the meals are reasonably lightweight, but some are lighter than others. When you choose your meals, you might want to know the approximate weight and bulk. These are the divisions we have used:

Under 1½ lbs/under 0.75 kg
1½ lbs to 2 lbs/0.75 to 1 kg
Over 2 lbs/over 1 kg

None of the dinners are very bulky. To help you select your meals and organize your packing, we have devised a four-level scale to rate the bulk of the dinners:

VERY COMPACT
COMPACT
MEDIUM
LARGE

Spaghetti with Vegetables and Tomato Sauce

This is an old favourite that we just had to include. It is also one of the first recipes we created! Serves 4.

Weight: 1½ to 2 lbs/0.75 to 1 kg *Bulk:* Large

For Tomato Leather:
  1 can (23.9 oz/680 mL) tomato sauce
  1 can (5.5 oz/156 mL) tomato paste

To Be Dried:
  12 to 14 mushrooms, thinly sliced
  2 large onions, slivered
  1 green pepper, julienned
  3 or 4 stalks celery, thinly sliced
  2 carrots, thinly sliced
  1 small zucchini, thinly sliced

½ cup (125 mL) potato flakes, commercially dried
2 to 3 tsp (10 to 15 mL) chili powder
½ tsp (2 mL) hot red pepper flakes
1 tsp (5 mL) each black pepper, oregano, dry mustard
  powder, and salt
2 cloves fresh garlic or powdered equivalent
1 tbsp (15 mL) soy sauce
1 lb (454 g) spaghetti
⅓ cup (75 mL) grated parmesan cheese (for garnish)

AT HOME:

- Whisk the tomato sauce and tomato paste together and prepare the tomato leather (see page 24).
- Prepare and dry the mushrooms, onions, green pepper, celery, carrots, and zucchini (see page 21).

PACK:

Tomato leather and spices in a plastic bag.

Each variety of dried vegetable and potato flakes separately in plastic bags.

Garlic in a plastic bag.

Soy sauce in a leakproof container (or in individual packages).

Spaghetti in a plastic bag.

Parmesan cheese in a plastic bag.

Wrap all of the ingredients in a labelled heavy plastic bag, with "At Campsite" instructions inside.

AT CAMPSITE:

- Rehydrate the dried vegetables, potato flakes, and tomato leather with the spices, soy sauce, and garlic in 6 cups (1.5 L) water in the large pot for about 30 minutes.
- Bring to the boil and cook for at least 30 minutes, stirring occasionally.
- Transfer the sauce to the small pot once it is cooked. (Remember that you will need a large pot to cook the pasta later. We recommend transferring the sauce to a smaller pot after it is cooked, as this works best with the size of pots that we use. But you might decide to cook the pasta in a smaller pot to avoid transferring the pot.) Keep the sauce simmering at the edge of the grill.
- Wash the large pot and half fill it with water. Bring to a boil.
- Add the pasta to the boiling water and cook until tender.
- Drain the pasta by placing a tea towel securely over the open pot. Keep your hands well away from the stream of water and the hot steam. Hold onto the edges of the tea towel and the sides of the pot as you tilt the pot towards the ground.
- Serve the pasta with sauce and garnish with parmesan cheese.

(If it is raining heavily, you can save cooking time by cooking the pasta directly in the sauce. First, make the sauce. Once the sauce is ready, add another 2 cups/500 mL of water and bring it to the boil again. Add the pasta and cook until the pasta is tender. This method is only barely satisfactory — it is definitely preferable to change the pots, as pasta will not cook through properly in a tomato-based liquid.)

VARIATIONS:

Spaghetti with Vegetables and Double Tomato Sauce
Cut 8 to 10 sun-dried tomatoes in pieces as desired, add to the pot, and rehydrate with the vegetables.

Spaghetti with Vegetables, Tofu, and Tomato Sauce
Slice a package of silken tofu into cubes. Add the tofu to the sauce about five to ten minutes before serving to warm through.

Spaghetti with Vegetables, Textured Vegetable Protein, and Tomato Sauce
Add ½ cup (125 mL) textured vegetable protein to the pot and rehydrate with the vegetables.

Spaghetti with Vegetables, Meat, and Tomato Sauce
Dry 1 lb (454 g) lean ground beef at home (see page 27). Add it to the pot and rehydrate with the vegetables.

STEW WITH DUMPLINGS

This traditional camping meal with fluffy dumplings covered with a thick vegetable sauce is requested repeatedly by the male campers on our excursions! Serves 4.

Weight: 1½ to 2 lbs/0.75 to 1 kg *Bulk:* Medium

For Tomato Leather:
  1 can (23.9 oz/680 mL) tomato sauce

To Be Dried:
  2 large onions, slivered
  2 carrots, thinly sliced
  3 or 4 stalks celery, thinly sliced
  1 cup (250 mL) frozen corn, thawed
  12 to 14 mushrooms, thinly sliced
  2 small zucchini, thinly sliced
  1 cup (250 mL) frozen peas, thawed

½ cup (125 mL) potato flakes, commercially dried
1 tsp (5 mL) each of oregano, dry mustard powder,
  pepper, and salt
2 tsp (10 mL) chili powder
1 bay leaf
3 cloves fresh garlic or powdered equivalent
1 tbsp (15 mL) soy sauce

2 cups (500 mL) biscuit mix, commercially prepared

At Home:
• Prepare tomato leather from the tomato sauce (see page *24*).
• Prepare and dry the onions, carrots, celery, corn, mushrooms,
  zucchini, and peas (see page *21*).

PACK:

Tomato leather, spices, and bay leaf in a plastic bag.

Each variety of dried vegetable and potato flakes separately in plastic bags.

Garlic in a plastic bag.

Soy sauce in a small leakproof container (or in individual packages).

Biscuit mix in a ziplock bag labelled with "add ½ cup (125 mL) water to the mix."

Wrap all of the ingredients in a labelled heavy plastic bag, with "At Campsite" instructions inside.

AT CAMPSITE:

* Rehydrate the dried vegetables, potato flakes, tomato leather, spices, garlic, and soy sauce in about 8 cups (2 L) water in the large pot for about 30 minutes.
* Bring to the boil and cook for at least 30 minutes, stirring occasionally.
* Prepare the biscuit mix, adding about ½ cup (125 mL) water to the ziplock bag and kneading slightly to combine.
* Drop the biscuit mix by spoonfuls, or squeeze out of the ziplock bag, on top of the boiling stew; cover immediately and cook for another 12 to 15 minutes. Don't peek!
* Serve and enjoy.

VARIATIONS:

Peanut Vegetarian Stew with Dumplings
Add ½ cup (125 mL) peanut butter and ½ cup (125 mL) peanuts to the rehydrated vegetables.

Tofu Vegetarian Stew with Dumplings
Slice a package of silken tofu into cubes and add it to the stew five to ten minutes before serving.

TVP Stew with Dumplings
Add ½ cup (125 mL) textured vegetable protein to the pot and rehydrate with the dried vegetables.

Beef Stew with Dumplings

Dry 1 lb (454 g) lean ground beef at home (see page *27*). At the campsite, rehydrate the ground beef with the vegetables and water for about 30 minutes. (You can also add beef in the form of beef jerky or dried beef and rehydrate as above.)

Stew with Biscuits or Dinner Rolls (instead of dumplings)

Prepare the stew as above, but use only 6 cups (1.5 L) water. If the stew must be thickened, gradually add ½ cup (125 mL) cold water to 3 tbsp (50 mL) flour. Stir to make a paste. Add some hot liquid from the stew and stir. Then gradually add all of the flour mixture into the pot; stir and simmer for a few minutes. Prepare biscuits (see page *120*) or serve with rolls or bread.

Moroccan Couscous

Even the most decorous people will find themselves licking their plates clean after this meal — giving in to peer pressure! Serves 4.

Weight: 1½ to 2 lbs/0.75 to 1 kg *Bulk:* Medium

To Be Dried:
  1 zucchini, thinly sliced
  1½ to 2 cups (375 to 500 mL) frozen green beans, thawed
  1 large onion, slivered
  1 can (19 oz/540 mL) chickpeas, rinsed and drained
  1½ to 2 cups (375 to 500 mL) cauliflower, thinly sliced
  3 to 4 stalks celery, thinly sliced

½ cup (125 mL) potato flakes, commercially dried
2 cloves fresh garlic or powdered equivalent
¼ cup (50 mL) dry cured black olives
1 jar (6 oz/170 mL) marinated artichoke hearts
1 bouillon cube or powdered equivalent
¼ tsp (1 mL) cayenne pepper
1 tsp (5 mL) each black pepper, parsley flakes, paprika, cumin, coriander, and salt
⅓ cup (75 mL) golden raisins
1 tsp (5 mL) turmeric
1½ cups (375 mL) couscous
⅓ cup (75 mL) sliced or slivered almonds for garnish

At Home:
• Prepare and dry the zucchini, green beans, onion, chickpeas, cauliflower, and celery (see page *21*).

PACK:

Each variety of dried vegetable, dried chickpeas and potato flakes separately in plastic bags.

Bouillon and spices in a plastic bag.

Garlic in a plastic bag.

Olives in a leakproof container.

Artichoke hearts and marinade in a leakproof container.

Raisins and turmeric together in a plastic bag labelled with "add to 1½ cups (375 mL) water."

Couscous in a plastic bag.

Almonds in a plastic bag.

Wrap all of the ingredients in a labelled heavy plastic bag, with "At Campsite" instructions inside.

AT CAMPSITE:

* In a large pot, rehydrate the dried vegetables, chickpeas, and potato flakes with the spices, bouillon, and garlic in 6 cups (1.5 L) water for about 30 minutes.

* Bring to the boil and simmer for at least 30 minutes, adding more water if necessary.

* Add the artichoke hearts with their marinade and the olives. Simmer for 5 minutes, stirring occasionally.

* In a smaller pot, boil 1½ cups (375 mL) water with raisins and turmeric.

* Five minutes before eating add couscous to the boiling water.

* Cover, remove from heat, and let stand for 5 minutes. Fluff with fork.

* Serve a spoonful of couscous on each plate. Top with vegetable sauce and garnish with almonds.

VARIATION:

Moroccan Couscous with Chicken

Add one package (1 oz/29 g) commercially dried chicken to the dried vegetables while rehydrating and proceed as above.

FRUIT AND NUT CURRY

This is the dinner that inspired us to create this cookbook. It is still a favourite meal and one that Bonnie often makes at home too. Serves 4.

Weight: 1½ to 2 lbs/0.75 to 1 kg *Bulk:* Medium

To Be Dried:
   1 green pepper, slivered
   3 to 4 stalks celery, thinly sliced
   2 large onions, slivered
   1 cup (250 mL) frozen peas, thawed

¼ cup (50 mL) potato flakes, commercially dried
½ cup (125 mL) dried apricots, cut into thirds
⅓ cup (75 mL) golden raisins
⅓ cup (75 mL) shredded coconut
½ cup (125 mL) cashews
1 tsp (5 mL) each of chili powder, cinnamon, cumin, black
   pepper, turmeric, coriander, and salt
3 to 4 tsp (15 to 20 mL) curry powder (may be adjusted to taste)
1 bouillon cube or powdered equivalent
2 cloves fresh garlic or powdered equivalent

2 cups (500 mL) rice
½ cup (125 mL) mango chutney (optional)
2 tbsp (25 mL) lime pickle (optional)

AT HOME:
• Prepare and dry the green pepper, celery, onions, and peas (see page *21*).

PACK:
Each variety of dried vegetable and potato flakes separately in
   plastic bags.

Dried apricots, raisins, coconut, and cashews together in a plastic bag.

Spices and bouillon in a plastic bag.

Garlic in a plastic bag.

Rice measured into a plastic bag labelled with "add to 4 cups (1 L) boiling water."

Small leakproof containers with mango chutney or lime pickle.

Wrap all ingredients in a labelled heavy plastic bag, with "At Campsite" instructions inside.

AT CAMPSITE:

• Rehydrate the dried vegetables and potato flakes with the dried fruits, nuts, spices, bouillon, and garlic in 4 to 6 cups (1 to 1.5 L) water in the large pot for about 30 minutes.

• Bring to the boil and simmer for at least 30 minutes. Stir occasionally and add water if necessary. The mixture should be fairly thick.

• In the smaller pot, boil 4 cups (1 L) water.

• About 20 minutes before serving, add 2 cups (500 mL) rice to the boiling water, cover, and simmer for 20 minutes.

• Serve curry over rice. Serve mango chutney or lime pickle on the side if desired.

SERVING OPTION:

- Serve with poppadoms (see page *123*). Prepare poppadoms while the rice is cooking. Poppadoms should be packed between two circles of cardboard, or between the plastic lids of margarine containers, to keep them from breaking.

With its colourful variety of fruits and vegetables, you'll be impressed by the great presentation. Serving poppadoms before (or with) dinner will also really impress your group!

CHILI

Canned beans dry very easily and regain their original colour and texture when rehydrated. You can substitute any combination of beans. Serves 4.

Weight: Under 1½ lbs/under 0.75 kg *Bulk:* Compact

For Tomato Leather:
  1 can (28 oz/796 mL) tomato sauce

To Be Dried:
  2 onions, slivered
  3 to 4 stalks celery, thinly sliced
  2 carrots, thinly sliced
  1 green pepper, julienned
  1 cup (250 mL) frozen corn, thawed
  1 can (19 oz/540 mL) kidney beans, rinsed and drained

1 bay leaf
1 tsp (5 mL) each of paprika, oregano, dry mustard powder,
  black pepper, and salt
2 to 3 tsp (10 to 15 mL) chili powder (to taste)
2 to 3 cloves garlic or powdered equivalent

AT HOME:
• Prepare tomato leather from the tomato sauce (see page *24*).
• Prepare and dry the onions, celery, carrots, green pepper, corn,
  and kidney beans (see page *21*).

PACK:

Tomato leather in a plastic bag.

Each variety of dried vegetable and dried kidney beans separately in plastic bags.

Spices and bay leaf in a plastic bag.

Garlic in a plastic bag.

Wrap all of the ingredients in a labelled heavy plastic bag, with "At Campsite" instructions inside.

AT CAMPSITE:

- Rehydrate the dried vegetables, kidney beans, tomato leather, spices, and garlic in 8 cups (2 L) water in the large pot for about 30 minutes.
- Bring to the boil and simmer for at least 30 minutes. If too thick, add more water. Stir occasionally to prevent sticking.
- Serve.

SERVING OPTIONS:

- Serve with rice (1 cup/250 mL).
- Spoon tomato salsa over each serving.
- Serve with biscuits or corn bread (see page *120*).

VARIATIONS:

Chili Con Carne

Prepare and dry ¾ pound (350 g) lean ground beef (see page *27*) at home. At the campsite, rehydrate the ground beef with the vegetables and tomato leather for about 30 minutes.

TVP Chili

At the campsite, add ½ cup (125 mL) textured vegetable protein to the vegetables and tomato leather, and rehydrate for about 30 minutes.

PASTA WITH CHEESE AND TOMATO SAUCE

Comfort food is always a hit. Here are some ways of adding more nutrition to an old favourite. Serves 4.

Weight: Under 1½ lbs/under 0.75 kg *Bulk:* Medium

For Tomato Leather:
  1 can (28 oz/796 mL) tomato sauce

To Be Dried:
  2 carrots, thinly sliced
  1 cup (250 mL) frozen peas, thawed

1 48-g package of commercially prepared powdered cheese
  sauce mix
1 lb (454 g) pasta (fusilli or macaroni)

AT HOME:
• Prepare tomato leather from the tomato sauce (see page *24*).
• Prepare and dry the carrots and peas (see page *21*).

PACK:
Tomato leather in a plastic bag.
Each variety of dried vegetable packaged separately in plastic bags.
Cheese sauce mix in its original package.
Pasta in a plastic bag.
Wrap all of the ingredients in a labelled heavy plastic bag, with
  "At Campsite" instructions inside.

At Campsite:

* Rehydrate the dried vegetables and tomato leather in 6 cups (1.5 L) water in the small pot for about 30 minutes.
* Bring to the boil and simmer for at least 30 minutes.
* Add the cheese sauce mix. Stir and cook for 5 minutes and leave to simmer while the pasta is cooking.
* Half-fill the large pot with water and heat to boiling. Add the pasta and boil until tender.
* Drain the pasta by placing a tea towel securely over the open pot. Keep your hands well away from the stream of water and the hot steam. Hold onto the edges of the tea towel and the sides of the pot as you tilt the pot towards the ground.
* Leave the pasta in the large pot and add the sauce.
* Stir and serve.

Serving Options:
- Serve with *Camp Coleslaw* (see page *118*) or *Carrot Raisin Salad* (see page *117*).

Variations:

Pasta with Cheese and Tomato Sauce and Wieners
　　Add a can of sliced cocktail wieners to the sauce. Heat through, stir, and serve.

Pasta with Cheese and Tomato Sauce and Tuna
　　Add one or two cans (6.5 oz/184 g) of drained chunk tuna when adding the sauce to the cooked pasta. Heat through, stir, and serve.

> To avoid attracting animals, take extra care in disposing of the water or oil drained from the tuna. Bury the liquid away from your campsite and wash the can thoroughly before flattening it to store in your garbage bag.

Spicy Lentils with Bulgur

This dish has great flavour, but is also one of the simplest to prepare. Serves 4.

Weight: Under 1½ lbs/under 0.75 kg *Bulk:* Very compact

For Tomato Leather:
  1 can (5.5 oz/156 mL) tomato paste

To Be Dried:
  1 onion, slivered
  12 to 14 mushrooms, thinly sliced
  1 cup (250 mL) frozen peas, thawed
  1 red pepper, julienned
  2 carrots, thinly sliced

2 cups (500 mL) dried red lentils
3 cloves garlic or powdered equivalent
1 tsp (5 mL) each cumin, cinnamon, black pepper, ginger,
  turmeric, and salt
¼ tsp (1 mL) each cloves and nutmeg
2 tsp (10 mL) paprika
½ cup (125 mL) bulgur
1 tbsp (15 mL) sesame oil

At Home:
• Prepare tomato leather from the tomato paste (see page *24*).
• Prepare and dry the onion, mushrooms, peas, red pepper, and
  carrots (see page *21*).

PACK:

Tomato leather and spices in a plastic bag.
Each variety of dried vegetable separately in plastic bags.
Lentils in a plastic bag.
Garlic in a plastic bag.
Bulgur in a plastic bag
Sesame oil in a small, leakproof container.
Wrap all of the ingredients in a labelled heavy plastic bag, with
"At Campsite" instructions inside.

AT CAMPSITE:

- Rehydrate the dried vegetables and tomato leather with the
  lentils, garlic, and spices in 8 cups (2 L) water in the large pot
  for about 30 minutes.
- Bring to the boil and simmer for at least 30 minutes.
- Add the bulgur and simmer for another 5 to 10 minutes. Bulgur
  will absorb extra sauce and make the dish thicker.
- Stir in the sesame oil.
- Serve.

SERVING OPTION:

- If you will be preparing this meal within the first three days, you
may want to bring a small container of plain yogurt (6 oz/175 mL).
Top each serving with a spoonful of yogurt.

CORN AND POTATO CHOWDER WITH HERB DUMPLINGS

Very hearty, this thick chowder is ideal for warming you up on a cool evening. Serves 4.

Weight: 1½ to 2 lbs/0.75 to 1 kg *Bulk:* Medium

To Be Dried:
   3 cups (750 mL) frozen corn, thawed
   1 large onion, slivered
   2 to 3 stalks celery, thinly sliced

1 cup (250 mL) potato flakes, commercially dried
1 package scalloped potatoes (commercially dried) with sauce
1 bouillon cube or powdered equivalent
2 cups (500 mL) biscuit mix
1 tbsp (15 mL) parsley flakes

AT HOME:
• Prepare and dry the corn, onion, and celery (see page *21*).

PACK:
Each variety of dried vegetable and potato flakes, scalloped pota-
   toes and sauce packaged separately in plastic bags.
Bouillon in a plastic bag.
Biscuit mix and parsley flakes in a ziplock bag labelled with "add
   ½ cup (125 mL) water to make dough."
Wrap all of the ingredients in a labelled heavy plastic bag, with
   "At Campsite" instructions inside.

AT CAMPSITE:

- Rehydrate the dried vegetables, potato flakes, scalloped potatoes with sauce mix, and bouillon in 8 cups (2 L) water in the large pot for about 30 minutes. Bring to the boil and cook for at least 30 minutes, stirring occasionally.
- To make herb dumplings: about 15 minutes before eating, add ½ cup (125 mL) water to the ziplock bag containing the biscuit mix and parsley. Knead lightly to make a dough.
- Now comes the fun part! Squeeze dollops of batter on top of the boiling chowder. Make one dumpling per person.
- Put the lid on the pot and cook for 12 to 15 minutes. Don't peek!
- Serve each dumpling with chowder spooned on top.

ASIAN-STYLE NOODLES WITH STIR-FRIED VEGETABLES

It is worth making this dish just to see the snow peas transform magically into bright-green parchment jewels when they are dehydrated. Serves 4.

Weight: Over 2 lbs/over 1 kg *Bulk:* Large

To Be Dried:
  1 onion, slivered
  1 red pepper, julienned
  1 zucchini, thinly sliced
  1½ cups (375 mL) snow peas

½ cup (125 mL) shiitake mushrooms, commercially dried*
½ cup (125 mL) lily buds, commercially dried*
3 garlic cloves or powdered equivalent

1 box (12.3 oz/349 g) firm silken tofu
2 tbsp (25 mL) sesame seeds
Rice noodles or rice stick (¾ of a 454 g package)*
Note: With the thick vegetable sauce, the 454 g package is too
  much. We suggest taking just ¾ of a package, or about 350 g.

SAUCE:
1 tbsp (15 mL) each of vinegar and sesame oil
2 tbsp (25 mL) soy sauce
2 tsp (10 mL) dried ginger
1 tsp (5 mL) salt (if desired)
2 tbsp (25 mL) all-purpose flour

* These ingredients are readily available at Asian food stores.

AT HOME:
- Prepare and dry the onion, red pepper, zucchini, and snow peas (see page *21*).

PACK:
Each variety of dried vegetable packaged separately in plastic bags.
Garlic in a plastic bag.
Flour in a plastic bag.
Tofu in its original, sealed package.
Sesame seeds in a plastic bag.
Rice noodles in a ziplock bag or a heavy plastic bag.
Vinegar, sesame oil, soy sauce and dried ginger together in a small, leakproof container.
4 sections of paper towelling for draining the vegetables.
Wrap all of the ingredients in a labelled heavy plastic bag, with "At Campsite" instructions inside.

AT CAMPSITE:
- Rehydrate the dried vegetables in 2 to 3 cups (500 mL to 750 mL) water in the small pot for 30 minutes.
- In a dry frying pan, toast the sesame seeds until browned (for 1 or 2 minutes); remove them from the pan and set aside for garnish.
- Boil water in the large pot for the noodles.
- Pour the water off the rehydrated vegetables and drain them on the paper towels.
- Heat a small amount of oil in the frying pan.
- Stir-fry the garlic, drained vegetables, and chopped tofu for about 10 to 15 minutes.
- Add the noodles to the boiling water, remove from heat, and let sit for 3 to 5 minutes (or as instructed on the package. Remember to check the package instructions before packing the noodles).
- In the small pot, combine 2 cups (500 mL) water, vinegar, sesame oil, soy sauce, ginger and flour. Stir to make a smooth paste. Add to the stir-fried vegetables in the frying pan and cook and stir until thickened — about 5 minutes.

- Drain the noodles by placing a tea towel securely over the open pot. Keep your hands well away from the stream of water and the hot steam. Hold onto the edges of the tea towel and the sides of the pot as you tilt the pot towards the ground.
- Serve the stir-fried vegetables and sauce over the noodles and garnish with the toasted sesame seeds.

SERVING OPTION:
- Spice up this meal with a dab of your favourite hot sauce.

LENTIL AND RED PEPPER STEW

The reaction to this meal was unanimous: "Wow!" Serves 4.

Weight: Under 1½ lbs/under 0.75 kg *Bulk:* Very compact

To Be Dried:
  2 large onions, slivered
  2 red peppers, julienned
  6 to 8 mushrooms, thinly sliced
  2 carrots, grated
  1 can (19 oz/540 mL) navy beans, rinsed and drained

1 cup (250 mL) dried red lentils
2 tsp (10 mL) each oregano, paprika, and chili powder
¼ tsp (1 mL) each cayenne pepper and black pepper
1 tbsp (15 mL) parsley flakes
1 tsp (5 mL) salt
1 bouillon cube or powdered equivalent
8 to 10 sun-dried tomatoes, cut into thirds
4 pita breads or other bread

AT HOME:
• Prepare and dry the onions, red peppers, mushrooms, carrots
  and navy beans (see page *21*).

PACK:
Each variety of dried vegetable and dried navy beans separately
  in plastic bags.
Lentils in a plastic bag.
Spices, salt, bouillon, and sun-dried tomatoes together in a
  plastic bag.
Pita bread or other bread in a plastic bag.

Wrap all of the ingredients in a labelled heavy plastic bag, with "At Campsite" instructions inside.

AT CAMPSITE:
• Rehydrate the dried vegetables and navy beans with the spices and lentils in 8 cups (2 L) water in the large pot for about 30 minutes.
• Bring to the boil. Cook for at least 30 minutes.
• Serve with pita bread or other bread of your choice.

SERVING OPTION:
- If you will be preparing this dish within the first three days, you might want to bring a small container of plain yogurt (6 oz/175 mL). Top each serving with a spoonful of yogurt.

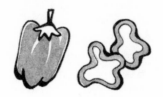

SOUTHERN PILAF

Colours abound in this easily prepared dish with a smoky, southern flavour. Serves 4.

Weight: 1½ to 2 lbs/0.75 to 1 kg *Bulk:* Very compact

To Be Dried:
   1 cup (250 mL) frozen peas, thawed
   1 cup (250 mL) frozen corn, thawed
   1 carrot, thinly sliced
   1 onion, slivered
   1 can (19 oz/540 mL) black beans, rinsed and drained

½ cup (125 mL) textured vegetable protein
1 tsp (5 mL) each thyme, oregano, paprika, black pepper, and chili powder
¼ tsp (1 mL) each turmeric and cayenne pepper
2 to 3 tsp (10 to 15 mL) spicy mesquite powder or liquid smoke
1 bouillon cube or powdered equivalent
¼ cup (50 mL) pumpkin seeds
8 to 10 sun-dried tomatoes, cut in thirds
¼ cup (50 mL) dry cured black olives
2 cups (500 mL) rice

At Home:
• Prepare and dry the peas, corn, carrot, onions, and beans (see page *21*).

Pack:
Each variety of dried vegetable and dried black beans separately in plastic bags.
Textured vegetable protein in a plastic bag.
Sun-dried tomatoes in a plastic bag.

Spices, bouillon, and pumpkin seeds in a plastic bag.

Olives in a small leakproof container.

Rice in a plastic bag.

Wrap all of the ingredients in a labelled heavy plastic bag, with "At Campsite" instructions inside.

AT CAMPSITE:

- Rehydrate the dried vegetables, black beans and textured vegetable protein with the pumpkin seeds, spices, bouillon, and sun-dried tomatoes in 8 cups (2 L) water in the large pot for 30 minutes.
- Bring to the boil and cook for at least 30 minutes. Stir occasionally.
- Add 2 cups (500 mL) of rice and olives to the pot of vegetables, cover, and let simmer on very low heat for 20 minutes.
- Fluff the pilaf with a fork and serve.

CREAMED TUNA WITH SHELLS

The rich and cheesy sauce makes this pasta very satisfying. Serves 4.

Weight: Over 2 lbs/over 1 kg *Bulk:* Large

To Be Dried:
    1 cup (250 mL) frozen peas, thawed
    3 to 4 stalks celery, thinly sliced
    1 large onion, slivered
    2 cups (500 mL) broccoli, thinly sliced
    12 to 14 mushrooms, thinly sliced

4 cups (450 g) small shell pasta
2 cans (6.5 oz/184 g) tuna
¼ cup (50 mL) green olives

Sauce:
2 tsp (10 mL) dried butter flavouring
½ cup (125 mL) all-purpose flour
¾ cup (175 mL) milk powder
1 tbsp (15 mL) parsley flakes
1 tsp (5 mL) each dry mustard powder, black pepper
½ tsp (2 mL) salt (if desired)
½ cup (125 mL) grated parmesan cheese

At Home:
• Prepare and dry the peas, celery, onion, broccoli, and
  mushrooms (see page *21*).

Pack:
Each variety of dried vegetable packaged in separate plastic bags.
Pasta in a plastic bag.
Sauce ingredients together in a ziplock bag.

Cans of tuna.

Olives in a small leakproof container.

Wrap all of the ingredients in a labelled heavy plastic bag, with "At Campsite" instructions inside.

AT CAMPSITE:
- Rehydrate the dried vegetables in 4 cups (1 L) water in the small pot for about 30 minutes.
- Bring to the boil and simmer for at least 30 minutes.
- Boil water in the large cook pot. Add the pasta and cook until tender — about 10 minutes.
- While the pasta is cooking, add 2 cups (500 mL) cold water to the sauce mixture in the ziplock bag and knead to make a smooth paste.
- Add the sauce to the vegetables in the small pot. Cook and stir until thickened. Cover and simmer for 5 minutes. Add more water if the sauce is too thick.
- Add the tuna and olives to the sauce. Stir and heat for 3 to 5 minutes.
- Drain the pasta by placing a tea towel securely over the open pot. Keep your hands well away from the stream of water and the hot steam. Hold onto the edges of the tea towel and the sides of the pot as you tilt the pot towards the ground.
- Leave the pasta in the large pot.
- Pour the sauce over the pasta shells.
- Stir and serve.

SERVING OPTION:
- Serve with *Carrot Raisin Salad* (see page *117*).

VARIATION:
Creamed Salmon with Shells
  Substitute canned salmon for the tuna.

APRICOT COUSCOUS WITH BLACK BEAN SAUCE

Instant black bean dip mix forms the base for this fruity meal. Serves 4.

Weight: Under 1½ lbs/under 0.75 kg *Bulk:* Compact

To Be Dried:
    2 carrots, thinly sliced
    1 large onion, slivered
    1 cup frozen corn, thawed

½ cup (125 mL) orange drink crystals
8 dried apricots, cut into thirds
¼ cup (50 mL) currants
1 tsp (10 mL) each cinnamon and ginger
½ tsp (5 mL) salt
2 cups (500 mL) couscous

Sauce:
½ package (1 cup/250 mL) instant black bean dip mix
1 tsp (5 mL) each chili powder, black pepper, and cumin

AT HOME:
• Prepare and dry the carrots, onion, and corn (see page *21*).

PACK:
Each variety of dried vegetable in separate plastic bags.
Orange drink crystals, dried fruits, cinnamon, ginger, and salt
    together in a plastic bag.
Couscous in a plastic bag.
Instant black bean dip mix with chili powder, black pepper, and
    cumin in a plastic bag.

Wrap all of the ingredients in a labelled heavy plastic bag, with "At Campsite" instructions inside.

AT CAMPSITE:

- Rehydrate the dried vegetables in 6 cups (1.5 L) water in the large pot for about 30 minutes.
- Bring to the boil and simmer for at least 30 minutes.
- Boil 3 cups (750 mL) water in a small pot and add the dried fruit, drink crystals, and spices.
- Simmer for 5 minutes. Add the couscous to the fruit and cover. Remove from the heat, and let sit for 5 minutes.
- In the meantime, add the instant black bean sauce mix and the spices to the cooked vegetables in the large pot. Cover, remove from heat, and let sit for 5 minutes.
- Serve the black bean and vegetable sauce over the apricot couscous.

Peas and Hard-Boiled Eggs in Cream Sauce

*Enjoy this meal within the first three days while the eggs are fresh —
comfort food is always a favourite with kids. Serves 4.*

Weight: Under 1½ lbs/under 0.75 kg *Bulk:* Compact

To Be Dried:
   3 cups (750 mL) frozen peas, thawed
   3 to 4 stalks celery, thinly sliced
   1 onion, slivered

6 hard-boiled eggs
4 slices of bread (for toast)

Sauce:
2 tsp (10 mL) dried butter flavouring
½ cup (125 mL) all-purpose flour
¾ cup (175 mL) milk powder
1 tbsp (15 mL) parsley flakes
1 tsp (5 mL) each dry mustard powder, black pepper, and salt
½ cup (125 mL) grated parmesan cheese

At Home:
* Prepare and dry the peas, celery, and onion (see page *21*).
* Hard-boil the eggs and leave them in the shell. (Store them in
   the refrigerator until you leave.)

Pack:
Each variety of dried vegetable packaged in separate plastic bags.
Hard-boiled eggs in an egg carton cut down to accommodate
   the number of eggs.

Sauce ingredients in a ziplock bag.

Wrap all of the ingredients in a labelled heavy plastic bag, with "At Campsite" instructions inside.

At Campsite:

- Rehydrate the dried vegetables in about 4 cups (1 L) water in a large cook pot for about 30 minutes.
- Bring to the boil and simmer for at least 30 minutes.
- Gradually add 2 cups (500 mL) cold water to the sauce mixture in the ziplock bag and knead to make a smooth paste. (If you are travelling with children, this is a great job for a child — very ooey-gooey!) Add the sauce ingredients in the ziplock bag to the pot. Cook and stir until thickened. Cover and simmer for 5 minutes.
- Peel and slice the eggs and add them to the creamed pea mixture. Stir and heat through for 2 minutes.
- Serve over toast.

Serving Options:

- Serve with *Carrot Raisin Salad* (see page *117*).
- Serve with *Camp Coleslaw* (see page *118*).

First-Night-Out Dinners

The first night out provides an ideal opportunity to have a meal with ingredients that may be more perishable or are bulky or heavy. If the drive to your destination is a few hours or more, use a cooler to keep perishable foods cool for as long as possible. Pasta salad, bean salad, and tossed salad are all good choices for the first dinner. Since you can't have fresh salad most other nights, you may want to savour it on your first night out. Fresh fruit for dessert is another wilderness treat as you won't be able to carry much of this heavy, perishable — and squishable — fresh food. Enjoy peaches, nectarines, or grapes on the first night — you won't be seeing fresh fruit for several days, unless there are berries to pick!

You can carry frozen meat in a cooler with an ice pack during your car journey. The meat will then thaw during the day and be ready to prepare for the first camp meal. Expand this meal with corn on the cob, baked or fried potatoes, rice, or stir-fried fresh vegetables.

VEGGIE BURGERS

*There are lots of options to keep this basic recipe ever-changing —
try them all! Makes 8 to 10 burgers.*

1 can (19 oz/540 mL) chickpeas, rinsed and drained
½ cup (125 mL) dried bread crumbs
1 onion, grated
2 medium carrots, grated (not chopped)
¼ cup (50 mL) sunflower seeds
2 eggs
2 tbsp (25 mL) tahini
½ cup (125 mL) fresh parsley, chopped finely
  (or 2 tbsp/25 mL parsley flakes)
1 tsp (5 mL) each oregano, turmeric, cumin, dry mustard powder,
  chili powder, and black pepper
2 tsp (10 mL) paprika
rolls (1 per person)
1 cup (250 mL) tomato salsa
¼ cup (50 mL) mustard

AT HOME:
• Lightly mash the chickpeas.
• Add the bread crumbs, grated onion and carrot, and the sun-
  flower seeds. Stir with a fork.
• In another bowl, combine the eggs, tahini, parsley, and other
  spices. Stir and add to the chickpea mixture. Stir thoroughly.
• Form into burgers. The burgers will be wet and fragile but will
  become quite firm when cooked.
• Bake on a greased baking sheet at 350°F (180°C) for 30 minutes.
  Cool on the baking sheet. Wrap individually in foil. Freeze extra
  burgers.

PACK:

Chickpea burgers, individually wrapped in foil (1 burger per person is usually sufficient).

Rolls (1 per person, as above).

Tomato salsa in a small leakproof container.

Mustard in a small leakproof container or individual serving packages.

Wrap all ingredients in a labelled heavy plastic bag with "At Campsite" instructions inside.

Label: "To be used the first night."

AT CAMPSITE:

• Place burgers on the grill in the foil packaging. Since they have already been cooked, they simply need to be heated through.

• Serve on rolls with tomato salsa and mustard.

SERVING OPTIONS:

- Serve with fried onions. Slice 2 to 3 onions. Sauté the onions in oil, until soft and slightly brown. Serve burgers with fried onions on the side.

- Serve with your choice of bean, pasta, or fruit salad; vegetables and dip; soup; baked potato (see page *115*); or corn on the cob (see page *116*).

VARIATION:

Falafel-style in a Pita

At home, make the *Veggie Burgers* recipe but shape into 1½" (3.75 cm) patties and bake them at 350°F (180°C) for 20 minutes. At the campsite, simply heat the falafels in a lightly oiled frying pan. Serve 2 to 3 falafels in each pita pocket with sliced cucumber and tomato. You might want to bring a homemade sauce made with 2 tbsp (30 mL) tahini, 1 cup (250 mL) yogurt, and 1 tsp (5 mL) cumin. Drizzle some sauce over the sliced vegetables and falafels in the pita pocket.

MEXICAN FIESTA

This meal is a bit bulky to carry but it works well for the first night out.

1 cup (250 mL) rice
1 large onion
1 small zucchini
1 green pepper
1 package instant black bean dip mix
1 large flour tortilla per person
1 cup (250 mL) tomato salsa
8 oz (227 g) of Monterey Jack or cheddar cheese, shredded

PACK:
Rice in a plastic bag labelled "Add to 2 cups of boiling water."
Fresh onion, zucchini, and green pepper.
Instant black bean dip mix labelled "Add 2 cups (500 mL) boiling water, cover and let sit for 5 minutes."
Tortillas in a plastic bag.
Tomato salsa in leakproof container.
Grated cheese in a plastic bag.
Wrap all of the ingredients in a labelled heavy plastic bag, with "At Campsite" instructions inside.

AT CAMPSITE:
• Bring 2 cups (500 mL) water to the boil.
• Add rice, cover, and simmer on low heat for 20 minutes.
• Heat oil in the frying pan. Slice and add the onion, zucchini, and green pepper and cook, stirring occasionally, for about 15 minutes.

- In another pot, boil 2 cups (500 mL) water and add the instant black bean dip mix and stir. Cover and let sit for 5 minutes.
- Fill the tortillas with cheese and stir-fried vegetables. Roll them up and top with salsa.
- Serve with rice and black bean dip.

SERVING OPTIONS:
- Serve with coleslaw.
- Serve with sliced avocado or tomatoes.
- Serve with pita bread instead of tortillas.

Nacho chips are an excellent complement to this meal. Bring some extra salsa to enjoy with the chips while you are preparing dinner.

VEGGIE TOFU KEBOBS

Choose your favourite veggies from the following: green or red pepper, green or yellow zucchini, cherry tomatoes, mushrooms, or eggplant. Veggie tofu kebobs served with rice and peanut sauce make a visually appealing and hearty meal.

Vegetables of your choice from suggestions above.
1 package (12.3 oz/349 g) extra-firm tofu (not silken)
2 cups (500 mL) rice

Marinade for vegetables:
2 tbsp (25 mL) rice vinegar
1 tbsp (15 mL) each oil and honey
1 tsp (5 mL) each dry mustard and ginger

Peanut sauce:
¼ cup (50 mL) peanut butter
1 tbsp (15 mL) soy sauce
1 tbsp (15 mL) all-purpose flour

AT HOME:
• Cut the vegetables into bite-sized pieces.
• Prepare the marinade for the vegetables. Combine oil, rice vinegar, honey, mustard, and ginger in a small, leakproof container.

PACK:
Fresh vegetables in a ziplock bag.
Extra-firm tofu in original packaging.
Rice in a plastic bag labelled "Add to 4 cups boiling water."
Marinade in a small leakproof container.
Peanut butter and soy sauce in leakproof container.

Flour in a plastic bag.
10 wooden skewers.
Wrap all of the ingredients in a labelled heavy plastic bag, with "At Campsite" instructions inside.

AT CAMPSITE:
- Cut the tofu into bite-sized pieces. Place the tofu and the marinade into the ziplock bag with the vegetables and let sit for 15 minutes. Turn the bag occasionally.
- Put 4 cups (1 L) water into the large pot. When boiling, add rice. Cover and simmer for 20 minutes.
- Assemble the kebobs and place them on the grill. Cook for about 15 minutes, turning once.
- To prepare the peanut sauce, mix the peanut butter, flour, and soy sauce with 1½ cups (375 mL) cold water in the small pot. Stir until smooth. Bring to the boil, stir and simmer for 5 minutes until thickened.
- Serve the kebobs on a bed of rice topped with peanut sauce.

SERVING OPTIONS:
- Serve with fruit salad or bean salad.

VARIATION:
If you are unable to have a campfire and can't grill kebobs at your campsite, revise the meal by preparing a stir-fry of the vegetables and tofu and serve this over the rice with the peanut sauce.

Quick Dinners

Stir-Fried Vegetables

If you will be using fresh vegetables, plan this meal for early in your trip. If you will be using dried vegetables, however, this meal can be served any time. To rehydrate the dried vegetables, add them to 2 to 3 cups (500 mL to 750 mL) water and let them sit for about 30 minutes. Pour off any excess water. Drain the vegetables well on paper towels or a tea towel.

Sauté the vegetables in a small amount of oil (from staples) in the frying pan. Serve in a pita pocket, or make a wrap sandwich with a tortilla or pita. (Heat your wrap by placing it over the almost-cooked vegetables in the frying pan. It will warm quickly. If you are heating several wraps, fill and fold the wraps and then place them in the empty frying pan until they are heated through.) Serve with salsa.

Variations:
Peanut Wrap with Stir-Fried Vegetables
Spread peanut butter onto the wrap before filling with vegetables.

Cheese Wrap with Stir-Fried Vegetables
Add some shredded cheese to the stir-fry filling.

Tofu Wrap with Stir-Fried Vegetables
Slice and add 1 package of tofu to stir-fried vegetables with 1 tbsp (15 mL) soy sauce.

Serving Options:
- Serve with soup, salad, or rice.
- Try adding toasted sesame seeds as a garnish. Toast the sesame seeds in a dry frying pan before sautéing the vegetables. Reserve the seeds until the vegetables are cooked. Sprinkle seeds on as a garnish.

INSTANT MAC AND CHEESE REVISITED

Cheap and convenient, packaged macaroni and cheese is remarkably high in nutrition with its cheese sauce and carbohydrate base. Finicky kids will almost always enjoy this dinner.

VARIATIONS:
Add tuna, salmon, or wieners to the prepared "Mac and Cheese."

SERVING OPTIONS:
- Serve with salad.
- Serve with veggies and dip.
- Serve with pita bread and fresh tomato and cucumber slices.
- Serve with stir-fried fresh (or rehydrated) vegetables.

GRILLED CHEESE SANDWICH

This "tried-and-true" favourite is for both the young and the young at heart.

• Make a cheese sandwich.
• Heat a small amount of oil in the frying pan and grill the sandwich on both sides until the bread is toasted and the cheese is melted.
• Serve with ketchup or salsa.

SERVING OPTIONS:
- Serve with salad, veggies and dip, or soup.

SIDE DISHES AND SALADS

Many people associate baked potatoes and roasted corn as classic camp foods. Some campers who depend on a meal or two of fresh fish serve these side dishes to round out the meal. We consider them extra treats because they are rather bulky, especially if you have a large group to feed.

Salad! We are *very* proud to present two authentic salads that can be served on any night — even day 7 of a week-long trip! As your last, cherished fresh produce items are consumed, you'll be delighted to munch on one of these quick-to-prepare rehydrated salads.

BAKED POTATOES

Heavy to carry, but delicious as a late-night snack or for lunch on a lazy beach day.

Potatoes, medium sized (enough for your group)
Cheese (optional)

PACK:
Potatoes.
Aluminum foil, measured (enough to wrap each potato individually) and folded into a square.
Small block of cheese.
Wrap all of the ingredients in a labelled heavy plastic bag, with "At Campsite" instructions inside.

AT CAMPSITE:
• Scrub the potatoes. Using a fork, prick each potato several times.
• Cover the potato skins with oil. Wrap the potatoes individually in aluminum foil. Place them on a bed of hot coals.
• Remove carefully after 45 minutes and check for softness. If they are still firm, return them to the coals for further cooking.
• Serve plain or add shredded cheese.
Note: If you don't have a campfire, you can slice the potatoes and pan-fry them with a small amount of oil. Stir until cooked — about 20 minutes.

Roasted Corn

Roasted corn is a classic campfire treat.

Cobs of corn in husks (enough for group)

Pack:
Cobs of corn in husks.
Wrap the ingredients in a labelled heavy plastic bag, with
"At Campsite" instructions inside.

At Campsite:
• Soak the unhusked cobs in water for 15 minutes and then drain
them. Roast the corn in husks on a bed of hot coals. Turn them
every 2 to 3 minutes. After 10 minutes, check to see if they are
ready.
• Husk, add salt (as desired), and serve.

Serving Options:
- Serve with soy sauce (Japanese style) or chili powder and lime
juice (East-Indian style).
Note: If you don't have a campfire, husk the corn and add it to a
large pot of boiling water. Boil for 7 or 8 minutes.

Carrot Raisin Salad

This rehydrated salad makes it possible to have a vegetable dish towards the end of a long trip when your fresh produce supply is dwindling.

To Be Dried:
  2 cups (500 mL) carrot, grated

⅓ cup (75 mL) raisins
1 tsp (5 mL) parsley flakes
¼ cup (50 mL) salad dressing of choice

At Home:
• Grate and dry the carrot.

Pack:
Package the dried carrot, raisins, and parsley in a ziplock bag.
Salad dressing in a leakproof container.
Wrap all of the ingredients in a labelled heavy plastic bag, with "At Campsite" instructions inside.

At Campsite:
• Rehydrate the dried carrot with the raisins and parsley in 1½ cups (375 mL) *treated* water for about 30 minutes.
• Drain off any excess water.
• Add the salad dressing and mix.
• Let sit for 10 minutes or until your meal is ready.
• Serve.

Variation:
Add 1 tbsp (15 mL) sunflower seeds.

> Children in particular will enjoy making this dish at the campsite because it doesn't involve heating but does involve rehydrating carrot, which is fun to watch.

Camp Coleslaw

Serve this rehydrated salad with many dishes to make meals even more substantial.

To Be Dried:
  2 to 3 cups (500 to 750 mL) cabbage, grated

1 tsp (5 mL) parsley flakes
¼ cup (50 mL) salad dressing of choice

At Home:
• Grate and dry the cabbage.

Pack:
Dried cabbage with the parsley in a ziplock bag.
Salad dressing in a leakproof container.
Wrap all ingredients in a labelled heavy plastic bag, with
  "At Campsite" instructions inside.

At Campsite:
• Rehydrate the dried cabbage with the parsley in 1½ cups
  (375 mL) *treated* water in a ziplock bag for about 30 minutes.
• Drain off any excess water.
• Add the salad dressing and mix.
• Let sit for 10 minutes or until your meal is ready.
• Serve.

BREADS

A good way to enlarge a meal to serve more people, or simply to satiate extra-large appetites, is to add biscuits, dumplings, or other bread products. The flavour and aroma of freshly baked quick breads will make any meal memorable.

After day six of your trip, you may be looking for alternatives to shrink-wrapped breads that are not as fresh as they were on the early days of your excursion. We've included *Biscuits*, *Chapattis*, and *Poppadoms*, which are all easy to carry and very simple to pre-pare at the campsite. No special equipment is needed to make these meal accompaniments. For the Indian breads you only need a frying pan; for the biscuits, you'll need a frying pan and a large pot. The biscuit recipe includes several variations, ranging from sweet to savoury.

BISCUITS

Once you've perfected cooking campfire meals, try baking biscuits. It really isn't as hard as you might think with your improvized oven!

2 cups (500 mL) biscuit mix

PACK:
Biscuit mix in a ziplock bag.
Wrap the ingredients in a labelled heavy plastic bag, with
  "At Campsite" instructions inside.

AT CAMPSITE:
- Gradually add ½ cup (125 mL) water to the biscuit mix in the ziplock bag and knead it to just combine. (Or add ½ cup/ 125 mL water to the dry mix in a container and stir with a fork.) If necessary, add more water.
- Drop the dough, in four equal portions, onto a well-oiled frying pan (or pot lid) by using a spoon or by squeezing the dough out of the ziplock bag.
- Put the clean, dry large cook pot upside down over the frying pan (or pot lid) to create an oven. Set on the grill about 6" (15 cm) from the bed of coals. If you are baking with a camp-stove, a heat diffuser can give more even heat distribution over the bottom of the frying pan.

- Bake for 15 to 20 minutes.
- Serve warm with dinner or for breakfast with jam, honey, or syrup.

Makes 4 large biscuits.

VARIATIONS:

Blueberry Biscuits:
Add ½ to 1 cup (125 mL to 250 mL) freshly picked blueberries and 1 tbsp (15 mL) sugar to the dough and bake as above.

Herb Biscuits:
Add 1 tbsp (15 mL) parsley to the dry mix.

Cheese Biscuits:
Add ½ cup (125 mL) shredded cheese to the dry mix.

Corn Bread:
Add ⅓ cup (75 mL) cornmeal to 1¼ cups (300 mL) biscuit mix.

Large Round Loaf:
Spread the dough evenly in the oiled frying pan to make one large round loaf. Cut the loaf into wedges when it is baked.

DESPERATION MEASURE:
If tops won't bake, use a flipper to turn the biscuits over. Cover and cook for about 5 to 10 minutes more.

Note: It is difficult to bake perfect biscuits while camping. Be careful that you don't let the fire become too hot or the bottoms will burn. A diffuser under the frying pan can help disperse the heat if a campstove is being used. With practice, you will succeed in creating delicious biscuits!

I once made biscuits on a beach in India for a group of British travellers. The fuel I used for the fire was dried cow patties. Believe it or not, this odourless fuel is perfect for creating the right level of heat. These biscuits were a huge success. — *Jill*

CHAPATTIS

Chapattis are an ideal bread to serve at the end of a long trip. They are easy to make, quick to cook, and just require flour and salt from your staples. Chapattis can be used as a bread with a meal or, more unconventionally, for breakfast with jam and peanut butter, or as a sandwich wrap for lunch.

2 cups (500 mL) whole-wheat or all-purpose flour
Pinch of salt

PACK:
Flour in a plastic bag.
Salt in a small leakproof shaker.

AT CAMPSITE:
- Put flour and salt into the large pot.
- Make a well in the centre and add ⅔ cup (150 mL) water.
- Mix with your fingers to make into a ball of dough. Add more water if needed. Knead the dough inside the pot for 5 minutes. Cover and let sit for 20 minutes (if you have time) to make it easier to work with.
- Divide into 8 portions.
- Roll or pat each portion into a round flat shape about 6" (15 cm) in diameter.

> You can come up with interesting devices to use as a rolling pin from your camping equipment. Patting each serving of dough with your fingertips also works well to flatten and shape the dough. I've seen camel drivers in India perform this process. The camel drivers also char the chapattis slightly by setting the cooked chapattis on a rock in the glowing coals. Whole wheat flour is the most authentic, but a combination of half whole-wheat flour and half all-purpose flour can be used. *– Jill*

- Heat the frying pan.
- Put one portion into the pan (without any oil).
- Turn after small blisters show on the surface.
- Press with a spatula to flatten. The total cooking time for each chapatti is about 2 minutes.
- Serve warm.

Makes 8.

POPPADOMS

These round, crunchy appetizers can be purchased in Indian food stores or in the international section of some grocery stores. They are sold as dry, flat circles in a plastic package. Choose from a variety of flavours, including the unbelievably hot "green chili" and pungent "garlic." Poppadoms are great for nibbling before dinner and are an excellent complement to a curry meal.

- Fry for about 1 minute each in the frying pan in 3 to 4 tbsp (40 to 50 mL) hot oil. Poppadoms curl up immediately when they are put in hot oil so hold them down with a flipper. Turn once and when they are cooked, set them on a plate to cool slightly before eating.

Note: To carry poppadoms in a food pack, sandwich the dried uncooked circles between two rigid cardboard circles or metal jar lids. Then package them in a plastic bag.

DESSERTS AND SNACKS

TO MAKE ON THE TRAIL

Satisfy your sweet tooth with a little dessert as you sit around the campfire. Admire the Milky Way, or, if you're lucky, a performance of northern lights. Now is the time to wrap your hands around a frothy mug of hot chocolate and exchange dreams with your companions. If your group is musical, this is the ideal time to sing along to a harmonica, mouth harp, or wooden flute. Sweet dreams ...

FRUIT DUMPLINGS

This is an extra-special treat when you find wild berries. Or you can bring your own dried fruit from home.

2 to 3 cups (500 to 750 mL) of any edible wild berry or 1 cup
    (250 mL) of any dried fruit or combination (apples, peaches,
    apricots, prunes, pears, blueberries, or cranberries)
½ cup (125 mL) plus 1 tbsp (15 mL) sugar
1½ cups (375 mL) biscuit mix

• Put the fresh fruit in the large pot with about 1½ cups water
  (375 mL) and ½ cup (125 mL) sugar. For dried fruit, add fruit
  to 3 cups (750 mL) water.
• As soon as the fruit mixture comes to the boil, add ½ cup
  (125 mL) water and 1 tbsp (15 mL) sugar to the biscuit mix,
  and knead to make a sticky, lumpy batter. This can be done in a
  ziplock bag. If using dried fruit cook the fruit mixture for an
  additional 10 minutes before adding dumpling batter.
• Drop by spoonfuls or squeeze the batter out of the bag over the
  bubbling fruit mixture. Make four equal portions.
• Put the lid on the pot and cook for 12 minutes. Don't peek!
• To serve, spoon the hot dumplings out onto plates and cover
  with fruit sauce.
• Makes 4 dumplings.

Chum, who usually has a small appetite, once had three
helpings of Blueberry Fruit Dumplings for dessert after a big
meal! We were amazed and, of course, have never let her forget that memorable evening.

We must confess that *Fruit Dumplings* is a recipe that we
have "tested" again and again with blueberries. Not that we
ever change anything, we just like testing it!   – *Bonnie*

Chum's Chocolate Birthday Cupcakes

Will someone be celebrating a birthday during your wilderness outing?
Surprise the birthday person — and yourself — with individual cup-
cakes topped with icing and candles!

½ package fudge chocolate-cake mix
16 chocolate wafers
• Most mixes require the addition of an egg, but we have success-
fully made these cupcakes many times without egg. You can add
1 tsp (5 mL) powdered egg if you like.

Pack:
4 aluminum foil muffin cups.
Chocolate-cake mix in a ziplock bag.
Chocolate wafers inside the stacked muffin cups, packed together
in a plastic bag.
Birthday candles in a plastic bag.
Wrap all of the ingredients in a labelled heavy plastic bag, with
"At Campsite" instructions inside.

At Campsite:
• Add ¼ cup (50 mL) water to the mix in a ziplock bag. Knead
the bag to mix.
• Pour into oiled foil muffin cups. Set cups into the frying pan.
Put about ½ cup (125 mL) water in the frying pan around the
cupcakes.
• Put the clean, dry large cook pot upside down over the lid (or
frying pan) to create an oven. Set on the grill about 6" (15 cm)
from the bed of coals. If you are baking with a campstove, a heat
diffuser can give more even heat distribution over the bottom of
the frying pan.
• Bake for 20 minutes. Try not to peek. Campfire heat is often too
hot for baking and the campstove heat source is often concentrated

into a small area. A diffuser will help distribute the heat more evenly for both methods of baking.

- When just firm to finger touch, remove from the heat and cool slightly. Put chocolate wafers on top to melt and form an icing.
- Add candles to suit the occasion and serve.
- Makes 4 cupcakes.

If you are having a surprise presentation, try to lure the birthday person away from the campsite. Otherwise the odour of chocolate permeating the campsite will ruin your surprise — especially if the birthday person has a nose for chocolate, like Chum! *— Bonnie*

CAMP CAKE

You can use many other cake mixes for a campfire dessert. Chocolate, white, spice, carrot, and gingerbread cake are some of the choices available. One package of cake mix will make a one-layer cake, which will fit in a greased frying pan to bake.

- Follow the directions for the cake mix.
- Pour the batter into a greased frying pan.
- Put the clean, dry large cook pot upside down over the lid (or frying pan) to create an oven. Set on the grill about 6" (15 cm) from the bed of coals. If you are baking with a campstove, a heat diffuser can give more even heat distribution over the bottom of the frying pan.
- Bake for 30 to 40 minutes. Check the cake occasionally to ensure that it doesn't burn. Be creative and add your own toppings, such as nuts or coconut (before baking), or chocolate wafers (after baking, melted on top).

Camp Coffee Cake

Use 2 cups (500 mL) muffin mix (several varieties available) with as much water as is required to make a stiff batter (approximately ¾ cup/175 mL).

• Pour the batter into a greased frying pan.
• Sprinkle with the topping (see below).
• Put the clean, dry large cook pot upside down over the lid (or frying pan) to create an oven. Set on the grill about 6" (15 cm) from the bed of coals. If you are baking with a campstove, a heat diffuser can give more even heat distribution over the bottom of the frying pan.
• Bake for 30 to 40 minutes or until firm to the touch.

Topping for Camp Coffee Cake:
½ cup (125 mL) rolled oats
¼ cup (50 mL) brown sugar
1 tsp (5 mL) cinnamon
¼ cup (50 mL) oil

Pack the rolled oats, brown sugar, and cinnamon together in a ziplock bag.
At the campsite, add ¼ cup (50 mL) oil to the contents of the ziplock bag and knead to make the topping.

Marshmallows

If the campers in your group are marshmallow fans, don't forget to pack half a bag or so to toast over the campfire before bed. Two or three marshmallows per person is usually enough. If they get too sticky in the bag to separate, you can add them to hot chocolate and call it dessert! Marshmallows are lightweight, but bulky, and they squish and melt easily. Enjoying a few on one evening is usually enough to satisfy a craving and evoke childhood memories.

TO MAKE AT HOME

As packing space is limited, it is important to choose snacks that provide a healthful addition to your diet — not just empty calories. We chose these cookie and bar recipes because they are nutritious and full of energy. They are also easy to pack and, of course, they taste great too. We have relied on Gramma's recipe files for many of these recipes. These snacks are favourites with afternoon tea at home as well as being superb trail accompaniments.

Firelighter Bars

These crisp bars are packed with flavour and are similar to granola bars.

½ cup (125 mL) butter or margarine
½ cup (125 mL) brown sugar
1 tbsp (15 mL) corn syrup
1 tsp (5 mL) vanilla
2 cups (500 mL) rolled oats
¼ tsp (1 mL) each baking powder and salt
2 tbsp (25 mL) sesame seeds
⅓ cup (75 mL) coconut

- Melt the butter or margarine in a large bowl in the microwave.
- Add everything else. Stir to combine.
- Press into a 9" x 9" (23 cm x 23 cm) greased pan.
- Bake at 375°F (190°C) for about 15 minutes, until bubbly and brown.
- Score in the pan while still hot from the oven.
- When cool, remove from the pan and break into bars.

Makes 8 bars. Store in an airtight container.
Prepare "snack packs" (see page *41*) when you are ready to go camping.

GRAMMA'S POWER COOKIES

*This Scottish recipe is a family classic. These oatcake "sandwiches"
with date-orange filling will satisfy mid-afternoon hunger pangs.
These cookie sandwiches keep for weeks if they are stored in an airtight
container in the refrigerator. Hide them well, however, as they are very
tempting when you need a power boost at home too!*

1 cup (250 mL) brown sugar
1 tsp (5 mL) salt
2 cups (500 mL) rolled oats
2 cups (500 mL) all-purpose flour
1 cup (250 mL) butter or margarine
½ tsp (2 mL) baking soda

Date-orange filling:
½ lb (225 g) chopped dates (about 2 cups)
½ cup (125 mL) cold water
grated rind and juice of 1 orange (or lemon)

Cookie mixture:
• Measure the brown sugar, salt, rolled oats, and flour into a bowl.
• Cut in the butter or margarine until the mixture is crumbly.
• Dissolve the soda in ½ cup (125 mL) hot water and add to mixture.
• Stir with a fork until a ball forms. Let sit for 20 minutes.
• Roll out on a floured board and cut into 2½" (6.5 cm) circles.
• Bake at 375°F (190°C) for about 10 minutes, until slightly browned.
• Cool on a rack.

Date-orange filling:
• In a small saucepan, cook the dates with the water, rind, and juice over moderate heat for about 10 minutes until thick and

smooth. Stir occasionally and add more water if it is too thick.
• Cool. (Date-orange filling can be stored in the refrigerator for
  two weeks.)
• Spread the filling onto one cookie and then press another cookie
  on top to make a "sandwich."
Makes 24 cookies.
Store in an airtight container.
Prepare "snack packs" (see page *41*) when you are ready to go
  camping.

Even exhausted campers can go for another hour or so
after a short break and a power cookie! These cookies were
given their name 25 years ago by a child who said, "Wow!
These must be power cookies!" Kids love the name "power
cookie." The cookies are tasty, but not too sweet, and they
do give you power.

SURVIVAL RATION SQUARES

These squares are quick to make and you won't end up with too many dirty dishes either!

1 cup (250 mL) butter or margarine
½ cup (125 mL) sugar
½ cup (125 mL) brown sugar
1 tsp (5 mL) vanilla
½ tsp (2 mL) salt
2 eggs
1 cup (250 mL) all-purpose flour
1 cup (250 mL) rolled oats
⅓ cup (75 mL) milk powder
⅓ cup (75 mL) bran
⅓ cup (75 mL) wheat germ
⅓ cup (75 mL) coconut
⅓ cup (75 mL) chopped nuts or sunflower seeds

- Mix the ingredients in the order given.
- Press into a 9" x 13" (23 cm x 33 cm) greased pan.
- Bake at 350°F (180°C) for about 20 minutes, or until light brown.
- Score in the pan into 24 squares while still hot from the oven.
- Cut when cool.

Makes 24 squares. Store in an airtight container.

Prepare "snack packs" (see page *41*) when you are ready to go camping.

GINGER COOKIES

These cookies are indestructible in your pack! We have nicknamed them "jawbreakers" — Gramma makes the best ones. For true jaw-breakers, don't substitute margarine for shortening!

1 cup (250 mL) shortening
2 cups (500 mL) brown sugar
1 cup (250 mL) molasses
1 egg
1 tsp (5 mL) vanilla
1 tbsp (15 mL) vinegar
4 cups (1 L) all-purpose flour
1 tsp (5 mL) salt
2 tsp (10 mL) each of baking soda, ginger, and cinnamon

- Cream the shortening, brown sugar, and molasses together in a mixing bowl.
- Add the egg and beat until smooth.
- Add the vanilla and vinegar. Stir.
- Sift in the dry ingredients and stir to combine.
- Chill for 4 hours (or overnight).
- Roll into balls about 1" (2.5 cm) in diameter and place on an un-greased baking sheet. Don't flatten; they will spread as they cook.
- Bake at 375°F (190°C) for 10 to 12 minutes.
- Cool on a rack.

Makes approximately four dozen cookies. Store in an airtight container to prevent them from softening.

Prepare "snack packs" (see page *41*) when you are ready to go camping.

CHOCOLATE WHEAT-GERM BARS

These rich fudgy bars will satisfy your craving for chocolate.

⅓ cup (75 mL) butter or margarine
1 cup (250 mL) brown sugar
2 eggs
2 tsp (10 mL) vanilla
3 tbsp (40 mL) cocoa powder
1½ cups (375 mL) wheat germ
1 cup (250 mL) rolled oats
½ tsp (2 mL) salt
1 cup (250 mL) chopped walnuts
1 cup (250 mL) chopped dates

- Cream the butter or margarine and brown sugar. Add the eggs and beat for 1 minute. Add vanilla.
- Add the dry ingredients and mix.
- Add the dates and nuts. Stir to combine.
- Spread in a 9" x 13" (23 cm x 33 cm) greased pan.
- Bake at 350°F (180°C) for about 25 to 30 minutes or until firm.
- Score in the pan into 20 bars while still hot from the oven.
- Cut when cool. Remove the bars from the pan and wrap them individually in waxed paper as they are a bit sticky.

Makes 20 bars. Store in an airtight container in the refrigerator. They will keep for several weeks.

Prepare "snack packs" (see page *41*) when you are ready to go camping.

Orange Apricot Bars

Here is an excellent alternative to expensive commercial energy bars — with a great fruity flavour!

⅓ cup (75 mL) honey
½ cup (125 mL) brown sugar
¼ cup (50 mL) oil
1 egg
1 orange, juiced, with rind grated
1½ cups (375 mL) rolled oats
1 cup (250 mL) whole wheat flour
½ cup (125 mL) wheat germ
¼ tsp (1 mL) salt
1 cup (250 mL) apricots, finely chopped
1 cup (250 mL) golden raisins
½ cup (125 mL) shredded coconut
½ cup (125 mL) sliced almonds

- Cream the honey and brown sugar. Add the oil and egg and blend. Add the juice and the rind from the orange and mix well.
- Stir in the dry ingredients. Add the fruit and nuts and stir to combine.
- Spread in a 9" x 9" (23 cm x 23 cm) greased pan and press to flatten.
- Bake at 350°F (180°C) for 30 to 35 minutes or until lightly browned.
- Score in the pan into 20 bars while still hot from the oven.
- Cut when cool. Remove the bars from the pan and wrap them individually in waxed paper as they are a bit sticky.

Makes 20 bars. Store in an airtight container in the refrigerator. They will keep for several weeks.

Prepare "snack packs" (see page *41*) when you are ready to go camping.

BUDGIE BARS

These fruit and seed bars have a great chewy texture and aren't too sweet.

1 cup (250 mL) butter or margarine
1 cup (250 mL) brown sugar
1 egg
1 tsp (5 mL) vanilla
1 cup (250 mL) all-purpose flour
1 tsp (5 mL) baking powder
½ tsp (2 mL) each cinnamon and salt
1 cup (250 mL) rolled oats
1 cup (250 mL) dried chopped apricots
½ cup (125 mL) raisins
¼ cup (50 mL) sesame seeds
¼ cup (50 mL) sunflower seeds
2 tbsp (25 mL) poppy seeds

- Cream the butter or margarine and brown sugar.
- Add the egg and vanilla and mix well. Sift in the flour, baking powder, cinnamon, and salt.
- Stir in the rolled oats, fruit, and seeds. Mix thoroughly.
- Spread in a greased 9" x 9" (23 cm x 23 cm) pan and press to flatten.
- Bake at 350°F (180°C) for 25 minutes until slightly browned.
- Score in the pan into 12 bars while still hot from the oven.
- Cut when cool. Remove the bars from the pan and wrap them individually in waxed paper as they are a bit sticky.

Makes 12 bars. Store in an airtight container.

Prepare "snack packs" (see page *41*) when you are ready to go camping.

MARSHMALLOW CRISPY SQUARES

These are a bit bulky, but are indestructible and keep very well. This recipe does not require baking and is a good choice for children who want to help prepare their own snacks.

¼ cup (50 mL) butter or margarine
About 30 large marshmallows
1 tsp (5 mL) vanilla
6 cups (1.5 L) Rice Krispies™

- Melt the butter or margarine in a saucepan over medium heat. (You can also do this in the microwave in a bowl.)
- Add the marshmallows and vanilla. Heat, stirring occasionally until the marshmallows have melted.
- Remove from the heat and add the cereal. Combine thoroughly.
- Press into a greased 9" x 9" (23 cm x 23 cm) pan while warm.
- Cool slightly and cut into 16 squares. Remove the bars from the pan and wrap them individually in waxed paper as they are a bit sticky.

Makes 16 squares. Store in an airtight container.
Prepare "snack packs" (see page *41*) when you are ready to go camping.

Peanut Crunch Squares

These squares can also be used for a nutritious breakfast for young children. This recipe does not require baking.

1 cup (250 mL) brown sugar
½ cup (125 mL) butter or margarine
½ cup (125 mL) corn syrup
½ cup (125 mL) peanut butter
3 cups (750 mL) Cheerios™
3 cups (750 mL) Rice Krispies™ or Corn Flakes™
½ cup (125 mL) chopped peanuts

* In a heavy saucepan, heat the sugar, butter or margarine, and corn syrup.
* Stir and boil vigorously for 1 minute.
* Remove from the heat and add the peanut butter. Stir until smooth.
* Add the cereal and peanuts. Mix well.
* Press firmly into a 9" x 9" (23 cm x 23 cm) greased pan while warm.
* Cool slightly and cut into 16 squares. When cool, remove the bars from the pan and wrap them individually in waxed paper as they are a bit sticky.

Makes 16 squares. Store in an airtight container in the refrigerator. They will keep for several weeks.

Prepare "snack packs" (see page *41*) when you are ready to go camping.

OTHER SNACKS:

- banana chips
- breakfast bars
- granola bars
- dried fruit (raisins, apricots, apples, pears, etc.)
- trail mix or "GORP" (Good Old Raisins and Peanuts!)
- jujubes or gummy bears
- hard candy
- nuts
- popcorn (bring kernels and use oil from your staples to make popcorn around the campfire)
- chocolate bars (wrap chocolate carefully so that if your chocolate melts, the rest of your pack won't become a sticky mess)

SUGGESTED MEAL PLANS

DESIGN-YOUR-OWN CAMP DINNER

Once you have tried some of the previous recipes you will likely want to experiment with other one-pot meal combinations. The chart on page *143* will help you create your own custom recipe and add more variety to your wilderness meals. The combinations are numerous. See where your own personal taste and experience will lead you — and have fun!

Choose your vegetables and fruits from *Group A* — pick 4 or 5 — keeping in mind that most dinners have some of the basics, such as onion, celery, green pepper, and then add additional vegetables of your choice. Choose sauce and seasonings from *Group B*. If desired, choose extra protein from *Group C*. Pick your carbohydrate choice from *Group D*. Choose the topping from *Group E*. Dehydrate, pack, wrap, and label as instructed throughout the book. You will have to determine the amounts for each item, which will vary depending on the appetites of your group. Use your own experience and the procedures from our recipes as a guideline to get you started.

GROUP A Vegetables and Fruits	GROUP B Sauces† & Seasonings	GROUP C Proteins	GROUP D Carbohydrates	GROUP E Toppings
- dried apricots	- cheese sauce	- beans (canned)	- cornmeal	- bacon bits
- artichoke hearts	- gravy mix	- cheese	- couscous	- dried seaweed
- carrots	- soup mix	- eggs	- pasta (choose type of pasta	- grated cheese
- cauliflower	- soy sauce	- lentils	to suit recipe)	- poppy seeds
- celery	- sweet and sour sauce	- meat (freeze-dried or	- potato	- pumpkin seeds
- coconut	- teriyaki sauce	dehydrated)	- rice	- salsa
- corn	- tomato sauce	- milk powder	- rice noodles or rice stick	- sesame seeds
- green beans	- white sauce	- nuts		- sliced almonds
- green or red peppers	- coconut milk	- peanut butter		- sunflower seeds
- mushrooms	- flavoured oil	- peanuts		- yogurt
- olives		- instant black bean dip mix		
- onions	- black pepper	- salmon/tuna/clams/sardines		
- potato flakes or dried slices*	- bouillon	- seeds		
- raisins	- chili powder	- textured vegetable protein		
- peas or snow peas	- curry powder, cumin,	- tofu		
- sun-dried tomatoes	and coriander			
- vegetable flakes*	- garlic			
- zucchini	- miso			
	- mustard powder			
	- oregano			
	- paprika			
	- parsley			
	- thyme			

* commercially prepared
† Lots of commercially prepared instant sauces are available.

GUIDELINES TO CAMPSITE PREPARATION

* Rehydrate the dried vegetables in 4 to 6 cups (1 to 1.5 L) water for about 30 minutes.
* Add the sauce and seasoning and extra protein, if applicable.
* Bring to the boil and simmer for at least 30 minutes. Add more liquid if necessary.
* Prepare the carbohydrate base and serve your custom-designed meal with the topping of your choice.

During dinner, you might want to ask everyone to choose a name for your meal and also brainstorm other possibilities for your next trip. Don't rule out your favourite at-home meals either, as many can be adapted for wilderness camping.

You will find lots of convenient products available at your local supermarket, natural food store, and international food markets. Some of the packaged meals are nutritious and you might want to supplement long trips by using some of the commercially prepared one-pot mixes. Alter meals by adding your own special ingredients and toppings. Check the directions on the package to see if you need to add anything other than water. Vegetables are often minimal in commercially packaged meals. With your dehydrating know-how, however, you can easily dry a variety of vegetables and add them to the mix. This will increase the portion sizes and will also produce a tastier and more nutritious meal.

Generally, packaged meals are more expensive than home-prepared ones. They can also contain more additives, fat, sugar, and salt. However, for quick weekend trips, you may enjoy the convenience of these meals if you don't have the time to do much "at home" preparation.

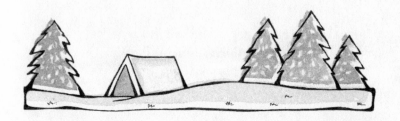

A VERY EASY WEEKEND TRIP

This model includes menus and shopping lists for a two-day trip for four people. It begins with Friday dinner and ends with Sunday lunch. This guide's main criteria is convenience. To save preparation time, you can take fresh produce, but this will increase the weight and bulk. For a three-day sample menu that incorporates more home-preparation time, see *A Three-Day Trip*, page *147*.

Menu for 2 breakfasts, 2 lunches, and 2 dinners

FRIDAY

DINNER
> *Veggie Burgers* (see page *106*)
> Salad

SATURDAY

BREAKFAST
> *Pancakes and Syrup* with Bananas (see page *62*)

LUNCH
> Tomato Herb Soup
> Bagels with Cream Cheese and Cucumber
> Apples

DINNER
> *Corn and Potato Chowder with Herb Dumplings* (see page *90*)

SUNDAY

BREAKFAST
> Instant Hot Cereal
> Toast with Peanut Butter and Jam

LUNCH
> Cream of Mushroom Soup
> Rye Bread, Cheese, Peanut Butter, and Jam
> Carrots

PLUS

Drinks (drink crystals, tea, coffee, hot chocolate)
Snacks (granola bars, trail mix, nuts, hard candy)
Staple Foods (oil, salt, pepper, ketchup/mustard/relish, peanut butter, jam, milk powder, white sugar, marshmallows)

SHOPPING/INGREDIENT LIST
FOR 2 BREAKFASTS, 2 LUNCHES, DRINKS, SNACKS, STAPLES

- Pancake mix – 2½ cups (625 mL)
- Pancake syrup – 1 cup (250 mL)
- Instant hot cereal – 6 to 8 packets
- Soup – 2 family-sized packages (serve 4): tomato herb and cream of mushroom plus 1 extra for emergency supply
- Bread – 4 bagels
    – 1 loaf rye, sliced
- Cheese – 1 package (8 oz/227 g) cheese
    – 1 package (8 oz/227 g) cream cheese
- Cucumber – 1 small
- Carrots – 4 to 6 medium
- Peanut butter – ½ to 1 cup (125 to 250 mL)
- Jam – ½ cup (125 mL)
- Tea – 8 to 10 tea bags
- Coffee – 1½ cups (375 mL) of ground coffee (this will make 4 mugs of coffee three times)
- Milk powder – 1 cup (250 mL)
- Drink crystals – enough to make 10 to 12 quarts (10 to 12 L) of juice
- Oil – ½ cup (125 mL)
- Hot chocolate – 8 to 10 individual packages
- Marshmallows – 12 to 18
- Apples – 4
- Granola bars – 1 package
- Nuts – 1 cup (250 mL) shelled peanuts
- Hard candy – ½ cup (125 mL)
- Trail mix – 1 cup (250 mL)
- Cookies – 1 package
- Bananas – 2

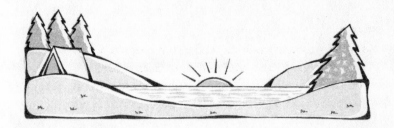

A Three-Day Trip

This model includes menus and shopping lists for a three-day trip for four people. It begins with the First-Night-Out Dinner, which you might skip if you eat at a restaurant on the way to your destination. The meal plan ends with Day Three Lunch, assuming you'll drive home after lunch on the last day.

Menu for 3 breakfasts, 3 lunches, 2 dinners, plus drinks, snacks, and staples

First-Night-Out Dinner
(skip this meal if you plan to eat at a restaurant)
 Mexican Fiesta (see page *108*)

Day 1
Breakfast
 Cream of Wheat with Cinnamon (see page *60*)
 Toast, Jam, and Peanut Butter
 Banana
Lunch
 Tomato Soup
 Bagels with Cream Cheese and Cucumber
Dinner
 Fruit and Nut Curry with *Poppadoms* (see pages *82* and *123*)

Day 2
Breakfast
 Pancakes and Syrup (see page *62*)
Lunch
 Cream of Broccoli Soup
 Rye Bread with Havarti Cheese, Peanut Butter, or Jam
 Carrots
Dinner
 Apricot Couscous with Black Bean Sauce (see page *101*)

DAY 3

BREAKFAST

Authentic Oatmeal Porridge with Raisins (see page 55)

Toast, Jam, and Peanut Butter

LUNCH

Cream of Vegetable Soup

Rye Bread with Cheddar Cheese, Peanut Butter

Carrots

PLUS

Drinks (drink crystals, tea, coffee, hot chocolate)

Snacks (cookies, trail mix, nuts, hard candy)

Staple Foods (oil, salt, pepper, peanut butter, jam, milk powder, white sugar, cinnamon, raisins, marshmallows)

SHOPPING/INGREDIENT LIST

FOR 3 BREAKFASTS, 3 LUNCHES, DRINKS, SNACKS, STAPLES

- Cream of wheat – ¾ cup (175 mL)
- Oatmeal – 1½ cups (375 mL)
- Pancake mix – 2½ cups (625 mL)
- Pancake syrup – 1 cup (250 mL)
- Jam – 1 cup (250 mL)
- Peanut butter – 1 cup (250 mL)
- Coffee – 2 cups (500 mL) of ground coffee (This will make 4 mugs of coffee 4 times.)
- Tea – 10 to 12 tea bags
- Drink crystals – enough to make 15 to 20 quarts (15 to 20 L) of juice
- Bread – 4 bagels
    – 2 loaves sliced rye bread
- Cheese – 1 package (8 oz/227 g) cream cheese
    – 1 package (8 oz/227 g) havarti
    – 1 package (8 oz/227 g) cheddar
- Cucumber – 1 medium
- Carrots – One 2-lb (907-g) bag
- Apples – 4 to 6
- Bananas – 4
- Soup – 3 family-sized packages (serve 4): tomato, cream of broccoli and cream of vegetable plus 1 extra package for emergency supply.

- Hot chocolate – 4 to 8 individual packages
- Marshmallows – ⅓ package
- Oil – ½ cup (125 mL)
- Hard candy – ½ to ¾ cup (125 to 175 mL)
- Trail mix – 1½ cups (375 mL)
- Nuts – 1 cup (250 mL)
- Cookies or bars – 3 "snack packs" (4 servings each)
- Raisins – ⅓ cup (75 mL)
- Milk powder – 1 cup (250 mL)

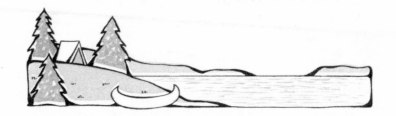

A Seven-Day Trip

This model includes menus and shopping lists for a seven-day, six-night trip for 4 people.

Menu for 6 breakfasts, 6 lunches, 6 dinners, plus drinks, snacks, and staples

Day 1

BREAKFAST (*at home*)

LUNCH (*You might have a car picnic on the way to your destination.*)
 Pita bread with grilled vegetables (grill at home), sliced tomatoes, black olives, and cottage cheese

FIRST-NIGHT-OUT DINNER
 Veggie Tofu Kebobs (see page *110*)
 Fruit Salad

Day 2

BREAKFAST
 Authentic Oatmeal Porridge with *Compote* (see pages *55* and *66*)

LUNCH
 Cream of Broccoli Soup
 Bagels with Cream Cheese and Cucumber

DINNER
 Moroccan Couscous (see page *80*)

Day 3

BREAKFAST
 Wholesome Pancakes with Syrup (see page *63*)

LUNCH
 Tomato Basil Soup
 Pumpernickel Bread with Hard-Boiled Eggs and Cucumber
 Apple

DINNER
Peanut Vegetarian Stew with Dumplings (see recipe "Variations" page *78*)

Day 4
BREAKFAST
Authentic Oatmeal Porridge with Raisins (see page *55*)
LUNCH
Cream of Asparagus Soup
Rye Bread with Havarti Cheese
Carrots and Apple
DINNER
Lentil and Red Pepper Stew (see page *95*)

Day 5
BREAKFAST
Creamy Couscous (see page *58*)
LUNCH
Cream of Snow Pea Soup
Linseed Bread with Peanut Butter or Cheddar Cheese
Carrots
DINNER
Spaghetti with Vegetables, Tofu, and Tomato Sauce (see recipe "Variations" page *76*)

Day 6
BREAKFAST
Authentic Oatmeal Porridge (see page *55*)
LUNCH
Tomato Vegetable Soup
Pumpernickel Bread with Swiss Cheese or Peanut Butter
Carrots
DINNER
Southern Pilaf (see page *97*)

Day 7
BREAKFAST
Instant Hot Cereal

PLUS
Drinks (drink crystals, tea, coffee, hot chocolate)
Snacks (cookies, trail mix, nuts, hard candy)
Staple foods (oil, flour, salt, pepper, peanut butter, jam, milk powder, white sugar, cinnamon, raisins, marshmallows)

- Instant hot cereal – 6 to 8 packets

Authentic Oatmeal Porridge (see page *55*)
- Oatmeal – 4½ cups (divided into 3 packages of 1½ cups/375 mL each)
- Raisins – ⅓ cup (75 mL)

Compote (see page *66*)
- Mixed dried fruit – 1½ cups (375 mL)

Wholesome Pancakes (see page *63*)
- Whole wheat flour – 1¼ cups (300 mL)
- Yellow cornmeal – ½ cup (125 mL)
- Powdered buttermilk – ⅓ tbsp (75 mL)
- Powdered egg – 2 tbsp (25 mL)
- Sugar – 1 tbsp (15 mL)
- Baking powder – 3 tsp (15 mL)
- Oil – 3 tbsp (45 mL)
- Salt – ½ tsp (2 mL)
- Pancake syrup – 1 cup (250 mL)

Creamy Couscous (see page *58*)
- Couscous – 1 cup (250 mL)
- Milk powder – 1 cup (250 mL)
- Prunes – 1 cup (250 mL)
- Brown sugar – ⅓ cup (75 mL)
- Cinnamon – 1 tsp (5 mL)
- Dried butter flavouring – 2 tsp (10 mL)
- Coffee – 4 cups (1 L) of ground coffee (enough to make 4 mugs of coffee 8 times)
- Tea – 30 tea bags (enough to make tea three times a day)
- Drink crystals – enough to make 40 to 44 quarts (40 to 44 L) of juice
- Bread – 4 bagels
  - 4 pita pockets
  - 2 loaves of sliced shrink-wrapped pumpernickel bread
  - 1 loaf sliced rye bread
  - 1 loaf sliced shrink-wrapped linseed bread
  - 1 loaf sliced shrink-wrapped multi-grain bread (extra)

- Cheese – 1 cup (250 mL) cottage cheese
  - 1 package (250 mL) cream cheese
  - 1 package cheddar cheese
  - 1 package (8 oz/227 g) havarti
  - 1 package (8 oz/227 g) Swiss cheese
- Eggs – 4 hard boiled (in shell)
- Peanut butter – 2 cups (500 mL) (this includes the peanut butter for the *Peanut Vegetarian Stew with Dumplings*)
- Jam – 1 cup (250 mL)
- Tomatoes – 2 medium
- Black olives – ¼ cup (50 mL)
- Grilled vegetables – 1 to 2 cups (250–500 mL)
- Cucumber – 2 medium
- Carrots – One 2-lb (907-g) bag (extra ones are for snacks or before dinner)
- Apples – 8 to 10
- Soup – 6 family-sized packages (serve 4): 1 cream of broccoli, 1 tomato basil, 1 cream of asparagus, 1 cream of snow pea, 2 tomato vegetable plus 1 extra package for emergency supply
- Hot chocolate – 10 to 12 individual packages
- Marshmallows – ½ package
- Hard candy – 1 cup (125 to 175 mL)
- Trail mix – 3 cups (750 mL) packaged in three 1-cup (250 mL) bags
- Nuts – 1 cup (250 mL)
- Banana chips – 1½ cups (375 mL)
- Cookies or bars – 6 "snack packs"
- Milk powder – 1 cup (250 mL)
- Biscuit mix – 2 cups (500 mL) (as extra or emergency supply)
- Sugar – 1 cup (250 mL) (for tea and coffee)
- Potato flakes – 1 cup (250 mL) (for thickening soups or dinners if necessary)
- Salt and pepper – small camp-style shakers

WILDERNESS CANOE TRIP CHECKLIST

This basic checklist is what we use on our canoe trips. The list of clothing is minimal as conserving weight is important, but it includes lots of layers to keep you comfortable and warm. It is helpful to read this list out loud to camping companions to make sure no one has forgotten any important items, such as a hat or sunglasses. The "Camping Equipment" list is also aimed at canoe trips, but many of the items are necessary for backpackers as well. The "Cooking Equipment" list will be effective for any type of camper. Even though this list is written for canoe trips, it is easily adapted for other types of wilderness excursions. Referring to the list will also help save you time in preparing for your trip. Personalize the list by adding items you may consider indispensible such as your bird book or that comfy camp pillow you bought last year.

Wilderness Canoe Trip Checklist

Clothes

- ☐ bathing suit
- ☐ hat
- ☐ lightweight long-sleeve shirt
- ☐ long pants
- ☐ rain gear/windbreaker
- ☐ running shoes/hiking boots/sandals
- ☐ shorts (1 or 2)
- ☐ socks (2)
- ☐ sweat suit (can double for sleepwear)
- ☐ T-shirts (2)
- ☐ towel
- ☐ underwear
- ☐ turtleneck jersey
- ☐ warm sweater or fleece top

Camping Equipment

- ☐ bailer (for canoe)
- ☐ bungie cords (2)
- ☐ canoe/paddles (one extra paddle)
- ☐ duct tape
- ☐ garbage bags
- ☐ grill
- ☐ ground sheet
- ☐ jackknife
- ☐ lifejackets (1 each)

- ☐ matches
- ☐ newspaper (a few sheets in a ziplock bag)
- ☐ backpack or canoe pack
- ☐ food pack
- ☐ rope x 3 (food pack, clothes line, canoe)
- ☐ saw
- ☐ sleeping bag
- ☐ tent
- ☐ underpad/sleeping mattress

OTHER

- ☐ _____
- ☐ _____
- ☐ _____
- ☐ _____

MISC. PERSONAL

- ☐ binoculars
- ☐ camera
- ☐ notebook and pencil
- ☐ paperback book
- ☐ sunglasses
- ☐ sunscreen
- ☐ toilet paper
- ☐ biffy trowel
- ☐ toiletries
- ☐ _____

EMERGENCY

- ☐ first aid kit
- ☐ flashlight
- ☐ I.D. in a ziplock bag
- ☐ insect repellent

- map and waterproof map case
- money
- whistle

COOKING EQUIPMENT

- aluminum foil (if needed)
- big spoon
- biodegradable dish soap
- campstove and fuel
- can opener (if needed)
- cook pots (set of 3 stacking pots with one lid)
- cups
- cutlery
- frying pan
- grater (if needed)
- knife (for cutting fruit and vegetables)
- pancake flipper (if needed)
- plates/bowls
- pot holder or oven mitt
- scouring pad
- tea towel for draining pasta
- water container
- water purification tablets
- _____

SAMPLE BASIC FOOD LIST

- apples/pears/banana
- biscuit mix
- bread
- carrots/cucumber
- cheese/cream cheese
- condiments: mustard, ketchup, soy sauce,

flavoured oil, cinnamon
- ❑ cookies or "snack packs"
- ❑ flour
- ❑ instant soup packages
- ❑ marshmallows
- ❑ milk powder
- ❑ oatmeal (or other breakfast choices)
- ❑ oil
- ❑ instant hot cereal packets
- ❑ assembled dinner packages (one for each night out)
- ❑ pancake mix/syrup
- ❑ peanut butter/jam/honey
- ❑ raisins/dried fruit
- ❑ salt & pepper
- ❑ sugar, brown and white
- ❑ trail mix/nuts/popcorn/candy

BEVERAGES

- ❑ hot chocolate
- ❑ drink crystals
- ❑ tea/coffee
- ❑ _____

RECIPE INDEX

SUBJECT INDEX